Enjoying Different

グローバル化の中で学ぶ日本文化

Arnold Arao
Kei Mihara
Yoshinori Miwa
Hiroshi Kimura

Nan'un-do

Download Audio

音声ファイル
無料 DL
のご案内

このテキストの音声を無料で視聴（ストリーミング）・ダウンロードできます。自習用音声としてご活用ください。
以下のサイトにアクセスしてテキスト番号で検索してください。

https://nanun-do.com　テキスト番号［**512074**］

※ 無線 LAN（WiFi）に接続してのご利用を推奨いたします。

※ 音声ダウンロードは Zip ファイルでの提供になります。
お使いの機器によっては別途ソフトウェア（アプリケーション）の導入が必要となります。

Read by

Rachel Walzer
Ryan Drees

※ Enjoying Different Cultures 音声ダウンロードページは以下の QR コードからもご利用になれます。

はじめに

本書はグローバル化の波の中で、世界における日本文化の魅力や価値を学び、未来を拓くときめきを提供します。観光や仕事、留学などで日本を訪れる多くの外国人は、日本文化に何を感じ、戸惑い、共感するでしょうか。来日する人たちは When in Rome, do as the Romans do.（郷に入れば郷に従え）という言葉を特に意識するでしょうが、彼らは日常生活から脱出し、日本で自国のものとは違う「非日常」を体験することになります。異文化理解とは、自国と他国の文化の違いを知るだけでなく、お互いの文化を尊重することで、その人たちの「心」を理解し、ありのままに受け入れることです。それによって新しい自分に出会うことになります。

筆者のアーノルド・アラオ氏はブリティッシュコロンビア大学とミズーリ大学で教育学を学んだ後、来日して小・中・高等学校で教鞭を取り、現在、大学で英語を教えている新進気鋭の研究者です。氏は日本文化に強い関心を持っています。氏の幅広い知識と研ぎ澄まされた鋭い視点で捉えた、日本と諸外国の文化を比較した 24 のエッセイはどれも興味深く、読む者の心を引きつけてやみません。

本書は英語の基礎をしっかり固め、「考える」英語力を身に付けることを目的とした、準中級レベルの英語総合教材です。英語の語彙や表現を単に「覚える」だけでなく、「考える」英語力を養うため、効果的に配置された練習問題を解くことで、リーディング、リスニング、ライティングの力をバランスよく伸ばすことができます。つまり、学生が自ら考え、問題を解決する思考力を養うことができるような形式で、主体的に無理なく英語に向き合えます。

本書の特長

1. 280 語程度の英文を読むことでリーディング力を強化
2. 語彙の意味、T/F 問題で本文の内容理解度を確認
3. 60 語程度の会話文でリスニング力をアップ
4. 80 語程度の空所補充問題で基本的な語彙、文法、表現力を定着
5. 英作文を完成することでライティング力を習得

本書を通して総合的な英語力を向上させ、日本文化と諸外国の文化の違いを楽しみつつ、自信を持って日本文化を外国に伝える国際人としての素養を身に付けてくれることを願っています。

2021 年 1 月
著者一同

本書の構成と使い方

「学生による授業評価アンケート結果」で気になることは、授業外学習時間が少ないことです。その点を改善し、主体的に学ぶ授業外学習時間を増やすため、全 24 ユニットで構成しています。つまり、15 回の授業に授業外学習のユニットを含めることで、学習時間を補うことができます。

1 Reading

エッセイを読んで、内容を理解します。

A Vocabulary

本文中の単語について、その意味を表す語句を選びます。

B True or False

(　　) 内の適切な語句を選び英文を完成します。次にその英文が本文の内容に合っていれば T (True)、間違っていれば F (False) を選びます。

2 Conversation

A Listen and Write

会話を聞いて空所に単語を書きます。

B Listen and Choose

質問を聞いて空所に単語を書き、最も適切な答えを (A) ～ (C) から選びます。

3 Text Completion

長文を完成するため、空所に入れる最も適切な語句や文を (A) ～ (C) から選びます。

4 Composition

A 日本語に合うように (　　) 内の語句を正しく並べ替えます。

B 質問に対する応答文を、(　　) 内の語句を使って自由に書きます。

Contents

Unit 1 College Sports

アメリカの大学では、バスケットボールやフットボールなどのスポーツは大観衆を魅了するだけでなく、大学の収入源にもなっています。日米のスポーツ文化の違いについて考えてみましょう。

1 Reading 2

Japan is not necessarily a country that is famous for its sports culture. Perhaps this is because Japan is better known for its other cultural artifacts like anime, video games, and digital devices, not to mention a long and storied cultural heritage that dates back approximately 1,700 years. Nevertheless, sports are an important part of modern-day Japan. This becomes obvious when one sees crowds of fans in team jerseys piling off a train after a baseball or soccer event, or all those students carrying around their kendo, kyudo, or baseball gear.

There are stark differences between sports in Japan and sports in the U.S., particularly when it comes to collegiate sports. Unlike in Japan, collegiate sports in America has an extremely strong and passionate fan base. Though university *Ekiden* races at the beginning of every year attract enthusiastic crowds, most Japanese sporting events do not compare to the extravagance and spectacle found at U.S. college basketball and football games. Part of the reason for this is that collegiate sports in the U.S. provide additional revenue for universities through ticket sales, merchandising, and donations. Therefore, it is important that college sports be as entertaining as possible so that fans will keep coming back for more.

Most college athletes do not go on to pursue athletics at the professional level. For them, college is the last place that they will experience the thrill of high-level team competition. Yet all college athletes, regardless of where their futures take them, share in the joy that comes from the deafening roar of their fans cheering them on during a championship match.

Notes **not necessarily**「必ずしも～ない」 **be known for**「～で知られている」 **not to mention**「～は言うまでもなく」 **date back**「～にさかのぼる」 **keep coming back for more**「何度も戻ってくる」 **go on**「～し続ける」 **regardless of**「～にかかわらず」 **deafening roar**「耳をつんざくような大歓声」

A Vocabulary

次の単語の意味を (a) ～ (g) から選び、下線上にその記号を書きなさい。

1. artifact ＿＿＿ (a) a set of equipment or tools
2. gear ＿＿＿ (b) an object that was made by people
3. stark ＿＿＿ (c) better than anything else
4. passionate ＿＿＿ (d) having or showing strong emotion
5. extravagance ＿＿＿ (e) money that is paid to an organization
6. revenue ＿＿＿ (f) the act of spending too much money on something
7. unrivaled ＿＿＿ (g) very obvious

B True or False

(　　) 内の適切な単語を選び英文を完成しなさい。次にその英文が本文の内容に合っていれば T (True)、間違っていれば F (False) を選びなさい。

1. According to the author, Japan does not (**necessarily** / **necessary**) have a strong sport culture. **[T F]**
2. Collegiate athletics in the U.S. (**are** / **is**) one way that universities can earn money. **[T F]**
3. Almost all college athletes eventually (**play** / **plays**) for professional sports teams. **[T F]**

2 Conversation

A Listen and Write 3

次の会話を聞いて空所に単語を書きなさい。

M: Hey! Did you catch the game yesterday?
W: No. I didn't. Who [1](　　　　　　)?
M: The Tigers [2](　　　　　　) the Carp in extra innings. It was a nail biter until the end.
W: Good for them. I didn't know you [3](　　　　　　) soccer.
M: I don't. They're [4](　　　　　　) teams.
W: Oh …

B Listen and Choose 4

質問を聞いて空所に単語を書き、最も適切な答えを (A) ～ (C) から選びなさい。

1. (　　　　) (　　　　) the man (　　　　　　)?
(A) He played a soccer match yesterday.
(B) He saw a baseball game yesterday.
(C) He loves animals of all kinds.

2. (　　　　)(　　　　) the man (　　　　) about the game yesterday?
(A) It was long and boring.
(B) It was long and exciting.
(C) He went home before the end.

3 Text Completion

次の文章を読んで、空所に入れる最も適切なものを (A) ～ (C) から選びなさい。

Almost 500,000 students participate in college sports in America. Participating in athletics _(1)_ many benefits such as improving health and making new friends. However, it also has unique challenges like increased anxiety and stress. Because college sports play a crucial _(2)_ in a university's success by bringing in additional revenue and increasing publicity, the pressure to win is intense. Many athletes attend college because they have received athletic scholarships. Without funding, _(3)_. Others see college athletics as the gateway to professional sports.

1. (A) have
   (B) has
   (C) had
2. (A) field
   (B) game
   (C) role
3. (A) I don't try or play as hard as I should
   (B) many are unable to continue their studies
   (C) you only watch sports on television

4 Composition

A 日本文を参考にして（　　）内の語句を正しく並べ替えなさい。

1. In the U.S., most of the earnings come (broadcast / from / popular / rights / the / to) football games on television.
   (アメリカでは、収益のほとんどは人気のあるフットボール試合のテレビ放映権から得られます)

2. The earnings (are / fund / other / reinvested / sports / to), improve facilities, and provide scholarships.
   (収益は他のスポーツに資金を提供したり、施設を改善したり、奨学金を与えたりするために再投資されます)

3. Students take (a way / as / compete / part in / sports clubs / to), have fun, and stay fit.
   (学生たちは競争したり、楽しんだり、健康を保ったりする方法としてスポーツクラブに入ります)

B （　　）内の語句を使って、質問に対する応答文を考えなさい。

1. What sports do you enjoy playing or watching?
   (I usually [often, sometimes] watch / Occasionally, I will)

2. Many people say that the government should do more to support amateur athletes. What do you think about that?
   (If the government wants / it should give / funding)

Unit 2 Homework

宿題が出されるのは、日本の学校ではごく当たり前のことで、教育上必要なものとされています。では、海外の小学生や中学生はどれくらいの時間を宿題にかけているでしょうか。

1 Reading 5

All Japanese students are familiar with homework. Homework is as commonplace as pencils and paper. When teachers fail to assign homework, it is often a cause for parental concern. Homework in Japan seems to be a requirement for education and a bane for students. The days before the summer holidays are always a time of dread for students, as teachers from each subject pass out homework booklets.

You may be surprised to learn, however, that Japanese students do not do the most homework in the world. That honor goes to students in Shanghai, who average 14 hours of homework per week! Russia is a distant second, with just under 10 hours. On the other hand, students in Finland spend only 3 hours every week doing homework!

In the U.S., teachers' attitudes toward homework have been drastically changing, and the amount of homework given to students can vary depending on the school. For example, many elementary schools expressly ban homework. On average, the U.S. junior high school student spends just over 6 hours a week on homework. This is a little higher than in the U.K. and France, where students spend about 5 hours a week on homework, which, by the way, is also the international average.

In comparison, at less than 4 hours per week, the amount of homework done by students in Japan does not seem so bad. Interestingly, much current research has examined the relationship between homework and academic success. What scientists and educators have begun to realize is that there is little correlation between how well students perform in school and how much homework they have to do. Rather, it is the quality of the assignments that they are given.

Notes **be familiar with**「～に慣れ親しんでいる」 **as commonplace as**「～と同じように当たり前の」 **pass out**「配る」 **a distance second**「大差の２位」 **by the way**「ところで」 **in comparison**「比較すると」 **academic success**「学業成績」

A　Vocabulary

次の単語の意味を (a) ～ (g) から選び、下線上にその記号を書きなさい。

1. assign ____ (a) a teacher; instructor
2. bane ____ (b) a cause of annoyance or unhappiness
3. vary ____ (c) distinctly; in a clear way
4. expressly ____ (d) study that is done to find new knowledge
5. research ____ (e) the relationship between things
6. correlation ____ (f) to differ in size, amount or degree
7. educator ____ (g) to require someone to do a task

B　True or False

(　　) 内の適切な単語を選び英文を完成しなさい。次にその英文が本文の内容に合っていれば T (True)、間違っていれば F (False) を選びなさい。

1. Homework is a (**natural / naturally**) part of Japanese education. **[T F]**

2. Many elementary schools in America do not give (**its / their**) students homework. **[T F]**

3. Research shows that doing more homework helps students (**improve / improved**) their grades. **[T F]**

2 Conversation

A　Listen and Write　6

次の会話を聞いて空所に単語を書きなさい。

M: Hey, Laurie. Missed you in class this morning. Everything okay?
W: Yeah. I was feeling a little under the weather and ^{1}(　　　　　) to sleep in.
M: Must be nice. Are you feeling ^{2}(　　　　　)?
W: A little, but I'm still a little out of it. I totally zoned out ^{3}(　　　　　) biology class.
M: Want to ^{4}(　　　　　) my biology notes?
W: That would be great. Thanks so much.

B　Listen and Choose　7

質問を聞いて空所に単語を書き、最も適切な答えを (A) ～ (C) から選びなさい。

1. (　　　　) was the woman (　　　　　) (　　　　) her morning class?
(A) She forgot she had a class.
(B) She had a doctor's appointment.
(C) She wasn't feeling well.

2. (　　　　) does the man (　　　　　) (　　　) do?
(A) Help the woman study.
(B) Lend the woman his notes.
(C) Take her to the hospital.

3 Text Completion

次の文章を読んで、空所に入れる最も適切なものを (A) ～ (C) から選びなさい。

Recently, there has been much debate about the value of homework. Though some studies indicate that _(1)_ there is a positive relationship between homework and student performance on unit tests, there is little evidence showing that homework affects overall academic achievement. Proponents of homework argue that homework helps _(2)_ learning. More importantly, they argue, _(3)_.

1. (A) because
   (B) though
   (C) when

2. (A) reinforce
   (B) strong
   (C) supporting

3. (A) it is better to reduce the amount of homework given to students
   (B) students must develop hobbies and other interests outside of school
   (C) homework helps students develop and use effective study skills

4 Composition

A 日本文を参考にして (　　) 内の語句を正しく並べ替えなさい。

1. Homework is meant (cover / in / learned / the students / to / what) class that day.
   (宿題は、生徒がその日授業で学んだことを補うためのものです)

   ____

2. In the U.S., (college homework / from / homework / makes / so different / what) in high school is that in college, there is so much more of it!
   (アメリカでは、大学の宿題を高校の宿題と大きく違うものにしているのは、大学でははるかに量が多いことです)

   ____

3. For an average student, (a large number / a shift / assignments / becomes / of / to) stressful and unbearable.
   (平均的な学生にとって、かなり多くの課題に移行することはストレスが多く、耐え難くなります)

   ____

B (　　) 内の語句を使って、質問に対する応答文を考えなさい。

1. Do you think you have too much or too little homework? Why?
   (These days [Nowadays / Recently], I feel as if / I am spending)

   ____

2. Recently, many educators assign students little homework or even none at all. What do you think about that?
   (The advantage / participate / extracurricular activities / The downside)

   ____

Unit 3 Tidying Up

日本では生徒が学校の施設を掃除するのは当然の習慣で、日々の教育活動の一環です。ところが、それは外国の人にとって、不可解なことの1つです。西洋では掃除をどのように考えているのでしょうか。

1 Reading

8

In Japan, the practice of cleaning the school is an integral and important part of students' daily lives. Though the practice is not nationally mandated, every school across Japan incorporates school clean-up, with little variation. Time is set aside for cleaning every day, and, for the most part, students and teachers alike actively participate in it without giving it a second thought.

In many Western countries, having students clean their schools and classrooms might be considered a form of child abuse. Rather, the cleaning and maintenance of the school falls on school janitors or contracted cleaning staff, who take care of these responsibilities after school hours. Moreover, students in the West often regard chores like cleaning as tedious and, in some cases, even punitive since they can be given in response to students' breaking school rules. There are also those students who would rather delight in defacing school property. In fact, in many countries outside Japan, graffiti and school vandalism are serious problems, often costing substantial amounts of money in repairs, not to mention creating the perception that the learning environment is unsafe for students.

Though foreign teachers working in Japan's schools may initially be shocked watching students tidy and mop classrooms, empty trash bins, and, especially, clean toilets, those teachers by and large recognize the inherent benefits of such activities. Students should be responsible for the areas they use. Having respect for their environment, practicing teamwork, and being responsible members of a community are all qualities from which all students – regardless of nationality – can benefit.

Notes **set aside**「取っておく」 **for the most part**「ほとんどの場合」 **give ... a second thought**「～を気に留める」 **child abuse**「児童虐待」 **contracted cleaning staff**「契約清掃作業員」 **in response to**「～に対して」 **not to mention**「～は言うまでもなく」 **by and large**「概して」 **regardless of**「～にかかわらず」

A Vocabulary

次の単語の意味を (a) ～ (g) から選び、下線上にその記号を書きなさい。

1. integral ____ (a) a person who cleans and takes care of a building
2. janitor ____ (b) a small job that is done regularly
3. chore ____ (c) boring or taking too long
4. tedious ____ (d) large in amount
5. deface ____ (e) very important and necessary
6. substantial ____ (f) to damage something, especially a public structure
7. empty ____ (g) to remove all the contents of

B True or False

(　　) 内の適切な語句を選び英文を完成しなさい。次にその英文が本文の内容に合っていれば T (True)、間違っていれば F (False) を選びなさい。

1. The way schools are cleaned is nearly (**a / the**) same in all schools in Japan. **[T F]**

2. For many American students, (**be / being**) asked to clean can be considered a form of punishment. **[T F]**

3. Foreigners teaching in Japan feel that having students (**clean / to clean**) the school is a waste of time. **[T F]**

2 Conversation

A Listen and Write 9

次の会話を聞いて空所に単語を書きなさい。

M: I'm sorry to disturb you, Ms. Hamm, but I was hoping you had some time to talk.

W: Sure, Linus. Come in. What can I [1] (　　　　　) you with?

M: I'm working on my paper about the differences between education in Japan and the U.S., and I was hoping you could [2] (　　　　　　　) some books or articles I could read.

W: I'd be happy to. But have you [3] (　　　　　) with Ms. Barski? She spent a few years in Japan, and I'm sure she would be willing to [4] (　　　　　) some of her own experiences with you.

M: No, I haven't, but that's a great idea. Thanks.

B Listen and Choose 10

質問を聞いて空所に単語を書き、最も適切な答えを (A) ～ (C) から選びなさい。

1. Why does the man (　　　　　　) the woman's (　　　　　　　)?
(A) To ask about his grades.
(B) To get some help for a paper he's writing.
(C) To talk about her stay in Japan.

2. Why does the woman (　　　　　　　　　) Ms. Barski?
(A) Because Ms. Barski is her friend.
(B) Because Ms. Barski teaches Japanese.
(C) Because Ms. Barski used to live in Japan.

3 Text Completion

次の文章を読んで、空所に入れる最も適切なものを (A) ～ (C) から選びなさい。

Many people are familiar with the sports brand ASICS; however, few people realize that ASICS is actually _(1)_. ASICS stands for *anima sana in corpore sano*, a Latin phrase which, loosely translated, means "a sound mind in a sound body." This expression was probably taken _(2)_ an ancient Roman poet who wrote, "You should pray for a healthy mind in a healthy body." This holistic view of health is a key element of modern education and is why _(3)_.

1. (A) a pseudonym
   (B) a synonym
   (C) an acronym
2. (A) away
   (B) from
   (C) off
3. (A) ASICS is a world leader in sports equipment
   (B) students spend so many hours studying
   (C) students are encouraged to participate in after-school sport activities

4 Composition

A 日本文を参考にして (　　) 内の語句を正しく並べ替えなさい。ただし文頭に来る語も小文字にしてある。

1. (charging / cleaning / students / the custom of / their own / with) classroom and school is unique to Japan.
   (自分の教室や学校の掃除を生徒に課す習慣は、日本独自のものです)

2. In the U.S., most schools (called / employ / employees / maintain / janitors / who) school facilities.
   (アメリカでは、ほとんどの学校が、学校の施設を維持する用務員と呼ばれる作業員を雇います)

3. In Western cultures, having children doing the cleaning in a school (a form / as / child / might be / of / viewed) abuse.
   (西洋文化では、学校で子どもに掃除をさせるのは、児童虐待の一形態とみられるかもしれません)

B (　　) 内の語句を使って、質問に対する応答文を考えなさい。

1. Many educators feel that cleaning the school helps students develop a sense of responsibility. Do you agree or disagree? Why?
   (I agree [disagree] with the idea that / because)

2. Some people believe that our environment directly influences our mental health. That is, if our environment is clean and ordered, we tend to be calm and steady. On the other hand, if our environment is untidy, we tend to be anxious and irritable. What do you think about that?
   (I agree [disagree] with the notion that / because)

Unit 4 School Schedules

日本の教育制度は、全国津々浦々まで同じです。アメリカでは州や町によって違い、高校でハイレベルな授業を受けて大学の単位を取得することも可能です。日米の教育制度の違いを考えてみましょう。

1 Reading 11

Elementary to high school education in Japan is standardized throughout the country. Whether students live in a large cosmopolitan city like Tokyo or in a small rural town, they have a very similar school experience. Japanese students attend classes five days a week, from Monday to Friday, with classes every other Saturday having been recently added to the school year. The Ministry of Education, Culture, Sports, Science and Technology (MEXT) determines the course of study, what subjects students will study, and the number of hours of study required for each subject. Schools then schedule these subjects accordingly throughout the week to meet MEXT's requirements.

Unlike Japan, the U.S. allows states and even school districts within states and cities to determine what students will study and how many classes they will take. Though students are expected to meet certain academic standards, the kinds of subjects and how often a student studies a subject can differ from state to state, and even from city to city. Moreover, students in the U.S. often study all of their required subjects every day. Because of this, a typical student's schedule has eight or nine periods of study each day with no mid-morning breaks. Moreover, especially in large schools, lunch can be scheduled at different times of the day for different students.

Another interesting aspect of U.S. education is the opportunity for students to participate in AP classes. AP, or Advanced Placement, courses give students the chance to experience introductory-level university courses; they can even earn credits for university classes while they are in high school! As Japanese universities face decreasing enrollment rates, it will be interesting to see if adopting practice similar to AP might encourage more students to pursue higher education.

Notes **every other Saturday**「隔週の土曜日」 **the Ministry of Education, Culture, Sports, Science and Technology (=MEXT)**「文部科学省」 **course of study**「学習指導要領」 **academic standards**「教育水準」 **required subject**「必修科目」 **mid-morning break**「午前中の休み」 **AP class**「AP クラス」高校で学ぶ大学レベルの授業 **enrollment rate**「入学率」

A　Vocabulary

次の単語の意味を (a) ～ (g) から選び、下線上にその記号を書きなさい。

1. standardize ____ (a) a part or feature of something
2. requirement ____ (b) a thing that is needed or wanted
3. district ____ (c) a unit that measures a student's progress
4. aspect ____ (d) an area of a county, city, or town
5. participate ____ (e) to change things so that they are equal or similar
6. credit ____ (f) to take part in an activity
7. pursue ____ (g) to try to get or achieve something over a period of time

B　True or False

(　　) 内の適切な単語を選び英文を完成しなさい。次にその英文が本文の内容に合っていれば T (True)、間違っていれば F (False) を選びなさい。

1. In Japan, the kinds of subjects and the (**require / required**) hours of study for each subject are determined by each school district. **[T F]**

2. States and cities in America have more (**choose / choices**) than cities in Japan concerning kinds of subjects students can study. **[T F]**

3. In America, some students can take university-level courses even before they graduate (**away / from**) high school. **[T F]**

2 Conversation

A　Listen and Write　12

次の会話を聞いて空所に単語を書きなさい。

W: Hey, Dan. Where are you going?
M: I'm heading to the library to study. I've got a biology exam in the third period, and I want to do some [1](　　　　　　　　).
W: Good luck on the test. Listen, I was wondering if we could meet today. I want to go over some ideas for the [2](　　　　　　　　) dance.
M: Sorry, can't. After biology, I have history with Mr. Hawkins.
W: Oh, okay. Well, [3](　　　　　　) does your schedule look like tomorrow? I'm busy, but I have a spare block [4](　　　　　　) French.
M: Sounds good. Meet you in the cafeteria?

	1	2	3	4	5
Tues.	Science	Spare	Biology	History	Drama
Wed.	Japanese	Economics	French	Spare	Writing
Thurs.	Algebra	English	Spare	French	History

B　Listen and Choose　13

質問を聞いて空所に単語を書き、最も適切な答えを (A) ～ (C) から選びなさい。

1. Why does the woman (　　　　　)(　　　) talk (　　　　　) the man?
(A) She wants to invite him to a dance.
(B) She wants to study biology with him.
(C) She wants to talk about some ideas about a school event.

2. Look at the schedule. (   )(   ) they probably (   )?

(A) Tuesday, 2nd period.　　(B) Wednesday, 4th period.　　(C) Thursday, 3rd period.

3 Text Completion

次の文章を読んで、空所に入れる最も適切なものを (A) ～ (C) から選びなさい。

In 1993, Anders Ericsson, a psychology professor, published a research paper on the practice habits of world-class violinists. What he found was that talent was only a part of _(1)_ made musicians proficient. What determined how successful people _(2)_ become was how much time they spent practicing. Ericsson concluded that the total number of practice hours required to become proficient was around 10,000. People, Ericsson noted, are not born great, _(3)_.

1. (A) that
   (B) which
   (C) what

2. (A) have
   (B) will
   (C) would

3. (A) and so they should quit as soon as something becomes too difficult
   (B) but may become great by the diligent practice of their craft
   (C) which makes talent the most important aspect of being successful

4 Composition

A 日本文を参考にして (　　) 内の語句を正しく並べ替えなさい。ただし文頭に来る語も小文字にしてある。

1. (a lot of / at / excitement / is / the beginning / there) of the school year, and students form many great friendships during this time.
   (年度初めはたくさんの刺激があり、この時期に学生は多くの親交を結びます)

   ____

2. In the U.S., many courses are (students / designed / for / take / them / to) in sequence and continue throughout the year.
   (アメリカでは多くのコースが、学生が順次履修できるよう計画され、通年続きます)

   ____

3. It is common for American students (at / majors / point / some / switch / to) in their undergraduate careers.
   (アメリカの学生にとって、学士課程のある時点で専攻を変えることはよくあることです)

   ____

B (　　) 内の語句を使って、質問に対する応答文を考えなさい。

1. What was your favorite subject in high school? Why?
   (When I / was really into / because)

   ____

2. Some people argue that Japanese students should study English more. What do you think about that?
   (If students studied / schools would have to / other important subjects)

   ____

Unit 5 Baths

日本人は家庭や温泉での入浴を楽しみますが、アメリカ人はシャワーを好みます。リラックスするための日本の風呂文化と、時間と水を節約するためのアメリカのシャワー文化について考えてみましょう。

1 Reading 🎧 14

Japanese people, in general, really enjoy their baths, whether at home or visiting one of the country's numerous hot springs or public bath houses. Bathing, for most Japanese, is an integral part of their daily routine. It is customary to clean yourself by pouring water on your body before stepping into a bath. In fact, the Japanese bathroom – both private and public – is designed around this practice, and space is provided next to the bathtub where people can rinse themselves off. Bathtubs are even "reheatable" so that the water can maintain a comfortable temperature for several hours. Moreover, it is not uncommon for family members to enjoy the same bathwater one after another. So it may surprise some Japanese to find out that for many foreigners, bathing is considered a luxury.

In America, for example, the majority of people prefer to take a shower, mainly because it requires less time and uses less water. Bathing is often considered a leisure activity, a time for soaking in a bubble bath while enjoying some peace and quiet. Communal bathing is mostly unheard of. Going to public baths like those at a Japanese hot spring would be considered exotic. In some other countries, particularly in Central and South America, many homes don't even have bathtubs, opting instead for shower stalls or cubicles. Because of the hot climate, many people take cold showers to cool themselves off.

Even after having spent much time in Japan, I still find that public baths, especially those in traditional Japanese inns, retain a sense of the exotic. At home, though I can appreciate the appeal of relaxing in a warm tub, my hectic schedule and the rising cost of utilities still make a shower much more sensible.

Notes **in general**「一般に」 **hot spring**「温泉」 **public bath house**「公衆浴場、銭湯」 **daily routine**「日課」 **pour water on one's body**「かけ湯をする」 **rinse oneself off**「体を洗う」 **one after another**「次々に」 **communal bathing**「共同で入浴すること」 **shower stall**「シャワー室」 **cool oneself off**「体を冷やす」

A Vocabulary

次の単語の意味を (a) ～ (g) から選び、下線上にその記号を書きなさい。

1. numerous _____ (a) able to be warmed again
2. reheatable _____ (b) gas, electricity, or water supplied by a town or city
3. soak _____ (c) shared or used by members of group
4. communal _____ (d) very busy
5. retain _____ (e) many; large in number
6. hectic _____ (f) to continue to have something; keep
7. utilities _____ (g) to take a long bath

B True or False

(　　) 内の適切な単語を選び英文を完成しなさい。次にその英文が本文の内容に合っていれば T (True)、間違っていれば F (False) を選びなさい。

1. Taking a bath is unique (**against / to**) Japanese culture. **[T F]**
2. Most people in America like to take showers (**instead / rather**) of baths. **[T F]**
3. Even after having (**lived / living**) in Japan for quite a while, the author still prefers bathing to showering. **[T F]**

2 Conversation

A Listen and Write 15

次の会話を聞いて空所に単語を書きなさい。

W: Hi, honey. I'm home.
M: How was your day?
W: Don't ask. I am just 1(　　　　　) it's over.
M: I'm sorry to hear that. Is there 2(　　　　　　　) I can do?
W: Thanks, but no. I'm just going to 3(　　　　　) in the tub for a while.
M: All right. While you're doing that, I'll get dinner 4(　　　　　).

B Listen and Choose 16

質問を聞いて空所に単語を書き、最も適切な答えを (A) ～ (C) から選びなさい。

1. (　　　　) (　　　　) the woman's (　　　　)?
   (A) It was a good day. (B) It was an okay day. (C) It was a bad day.
2. What does the woman (　　　　) the man (　　　) (　　　)?
   (A) Make lunch. (B) Nothing. (C) Take a bath.

3 Text Completion

次の文章を読んで、空所に入れる最も適切な語句や文を (A) ～ (C) から選びなさい。

The most enjoyable thing about taking a bath is the temperature. However, after a while, the water starts to cool down. Some people add hot water to _(1)_ the temperature. With our new self-heating bathtub, all you have to do _(2)_ a button. Pushing the reheat button recirculates and reheats the water in your tub so you can enjoy your bath for as long as you like. _(3)_

1. (A) arise
   (B) raise
   (C) rise

2. (A) are to push
   (B) is push
   (C) will push

3. (A) This, of course, increases the cost of utilities.
   (B) Heat the tub by pushing the reheat button.
   (C) Our self-heating bathtub makes bathing easy and enjoyable.

4 Composition

A 日本文を参考にして (　　) 内の語句を正しく並べ替えなさい。

1. The majority of Japanese take a bath at night before going to bed, but in the U.S., (before / leaving / many people / prefer / shower / to) the house in the morning.
   (日本人の大半は夜寝る前に風呂に入りますが、アメリカでは多くの人が朝家を出る前にシャワーを浴びるのを好みます)

2. Americans prefer showers mainly to save time, but for Japanese, (having / greater way / no / than / there's / to relax) a soak in a hot bath.
   (アメリカ人は主に時間を節約するためにシャワーを好みますが、日本人にとって温かい風呂に浸かるよりもリラックスする素晴らしい方法はありません)

3. Most Americans take showers to get clean, but Japanese think of the bath (as / away / the place / their daily / to / wash) fatigue.
   (ほとんどのアメリカ人は体をきれいにするためにシャワーを浴びますが、日本人は風呂を1日の疲れを洗い流す場と考えます)

B (　　) 内の語句を使って、質問に対する応答文を考えなさい。

1. Do you prefer taking a bath or taking a shower? Why?
   (prefer A to B / because)

2. Some people say that Japanese are not as concerned about environmental issues as people from other countries. What do you think about that?
   (not only / separate burnable from / but there are also / recycle)

Unit 6 Mamachari

ママチャリは今や、特徴的な日本文化の１つになっていると言っても過言ではありません。子どもを乗せるだけでなく、買い物や通勤通学にも使用します。最近では外国でも人気が出ている、頼りになるママチャリについて考えてみましょう。

1 Reading 17

On any street in Japan, whether in a large city or in the rural countryside, you will undoubtedly come across one of Japan's quirkiest features – the mamachari. Recognizable for their unique design, the mamachari are ubiquitous, used by anyone regardless of age, gender, or occupation. They are used to haul groceries, transport children, and commute to work or school. In a country where 85% of the population own bicycles, the mamachari, first produced in the 1950s, is the bicycle of choice. Nowadays, the iconic mamachari can be customized to suit your particular needs. You can choose your favorite color and add on baskets, mudguards, and up to two child seats. You can also add specialized holders for phones, coffee mugs, and umbrellas! In 1993, the first electric-assisted bicycle was produced, and now almost all new mamachari come equipped with electric motors.

Unlike other parts of the world where bicycles are primarily recreational – used for climbing mountain trails, racing, grabbing air, and doing tricks – the mamachari are primarily utilitarian. They are the equivalent of the American station wagon. That said, the mamachari are also extremely versatile, and there is even an annual Mamachari Endurance Race that draws thousands of spectators! The uniqueness of the mamachari has created some interest abroad. In 2013, the first mamachari bicycle store opened in London. In some developing countries in Africa, the mamachari have gained popularity because of their affordability, ruggedness, and reliability.

I enjoy cycling as a hobby and own a few high-end bicycles. But when it comes to running errands or commuting to work, the mamachari is my go-to bike to get the job done.

Notes **regardless of**「～にかかわらず」 **of choice**「一般に好まれる」 **electric-assisted bicycle**「電動自転車」 **come equipped with**「～が装備されている」 **grab air**「（空中に）ジャンプする」 **do a trick**「曲乗りをする」 **That said**「つまり」 **Mamachari Endurance Race**「ママチャリ耐久レース」 **high-end**「高級な」 **go-to**「頼りになる」

A Vocabulary

次の単語の意味を (a) ～ (g) から選び、下線上にその記号を書きなさい。

1. quirky ＿＿＿ (a) having many different uses
2. ubiquitous ＿＿＿ (b) having the same value
3. occupation ＿＿＿ (c) seeming to be seen or found everywhere
4. haul ＿＿＿ (d) strange, odd, or weird
5. customize ＿＿＿ (e) the work that a person does; a job
6. equivalent ＿＿＿ (f) to change something in order to fit a specific use
7. versatile ＿＿＿ (g) to move or carrying something

B True or False

(　　) 内の適切な単語を選び英文を完成しなさい。次にその英文が本文の内容に合っていれば T (True)、間違っていれば F (False) を選びなさい。

1. The mamachari bicycle has not changed at all (**from / since**) its inception in the 1950s. **[T F]**

2. In Western countries, bicycles are (**most / mostly**) used to run errands. **[T F]**

3. For daily activities, the author prefers to use high-end bicycles rather (**than / to**) mamachari. **[T F]**

2 Conversation

A Listen and Write 18

次の会話を聞いて空所に単語を書きなさい。

M: Hey, look at this! Cycle Shop is having a clearance sale!
W: Really? What was it you were [1](　　　　　) for? A road bike?
M: Actually, I'm still on the fence. [2](　　　　　) that or a mountain bike.
W: What do you want to use it for?
M: Commuting to school, of course, but I was also thinking that it would be fun to [3](　　　　　) some trails on my days off. The bikes are just so expensive, though.
W: Well, it says here that mountain bikes are [4](　　　　　) percent off! How about going to the store and having a look around?

B Listen and Choose 19

質問を聞いて空所に単語を書き、最も適切な答えを (A) ～ (C) から選びなさい。

1. What (　　　　)(　　　　) bicycle does the man want to (　　　　)?
(A) A mountain bike. (B) A road bike. (C) He hasn't decided.

2. What does the man want to (　　　　)(　　　　) bicycle (　　　　)?
(A) For recreation. (B) To go to school. (C) Both recreation and going to school.

3 Text Completion

次の文章を読んで、空所に入れる最も適切なものを (A) ～ (C) から選びなさい。

Nowadays, more people are looking at electric bicycles as a _(1)_ way of speeding up their commutes. Many people are turned off by the bikes' large external batteries. However, recent advances have _(2)_ engineers to design smaller, more powerful batteries. There have also been dramatic changes to bicycle design. There is even a new folding electric bike that can be stored in the trunk of your car. The stronger appeal to consumers, combined with newer bicycles' ability to travel longer distances more easily, means that _(3)_.

1. (A) convenience
   (B) convenient
   (C) conveniently

2. (A) allowed
   (B) let
   (C) made

3. (A) electric bikes are not practical for everyday commuting
   (B) electric bikes will only be used for short trips in the city
   (C) electric bikes will only continue to grow in popularity

4 Composition

A 日本文を参考にして (　　) 内の語句を正しく並べ替えなさい。

1. Mamachari is a (Japanese words, / "mama" / mash-up / meaning mother / of / two), and "chari" a slang word for bicycle.
   (ママチャリは母を意味する「ママ」と、自転車の俗語である「チャリ」の２つの日本語の単語を組み合わせたものです)

   ____

2. The mamachari have (being / beyond / for / gone / merely bicycles / mothers) to become bikes for men and women of all ages.
   (ママチャリは単なる母親用の自転車を超えて、あらゆる年齢の男女の自転車になりました)

   ____

3. As the mamachari continue to gain admirers abroad, you may one day (around / in cities / rolling down / see / streets / it) the globe.
   (ママチャリは海外でファンを増やし続けているので、いつかそれが世界中の都市の通りを走っているのを見るかもしれません)

   ____

B (　　) 内の語句を使って、質問に対する応答文を考えなさい。

1. Where you live in Japan, do you think it is really necessary to own a car? Why or why not?
   (case-by-case basis / activities / accessibility to trains)

   ____

2. Do you think that non-traditional modes of transportation like electric vehicles will become more or less popular in the future? Why or why not?
   (As gas becomes / non-traditional transportation / popular)

   ____

Unit 7 Vegetarian Diet

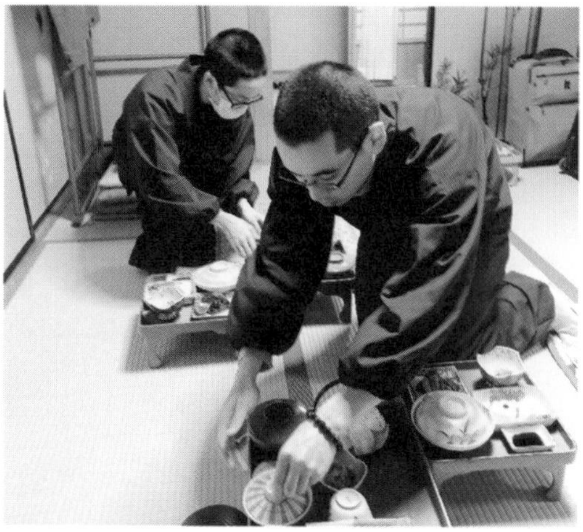

精進料理は西洋のベジタリアンフードに近いものですが、日本でベジタリアンに優しい料理を見つけるのは難しいと言われます。一方、西洋では食べ物に様々な配慮がなされています。ベジタリアンとビーガンの違いなどについても考えてみましょう。

1 Reading 20

Known for its aesthetically pleasing and simple, natural cooking style, Japanese cuisine would seem to lend itself naturally to a vegetarian diet. However, it is very difficult to find food in Japan that is vegetarian, much less vegan. Even the seemingly innocuous "dashi," which is found in many dishes, is made from dried tuna shavings. In addition, there is the ubiquitous and liberal use of dried bonito flakes as toppings for soups and other dishes. Even the canned, iced coffee jelly that is so popular in the summer is made from animal-based gelatin.

In the West, vegetarians abstain from eating meat or fish; vegans do not eat or use any products that come from any animals. For the most part, people choose to become vegetarian or vegan for religious, health, or ideological reasons. Thus, this lifestyle is highly personal and significant to the individual. Perhaps because of the prevalence of fish in the Japanese diet, or because of the belief that meat is an important staple of any diet, vegetarianism is not widely practiced in Japan. In fact, the Japanese tend to have a much more forgiving definition of vegetarianism. Japanese vegetarians often have fish, eggs, and fish-and-egg by-products as part of many meals. In fact, the closest counterpart to Western vegetarianism in Japan is "shojin ryori," or devotional cuisine, which uses only parts of plants without destroying the stem.

Although it is difficult to find truly vegetarian food in Japan, it is by no means impossible, and the effort used to find vegetarian friendly dishes results in wonderful and interesting interactions with the people and the culture.

Notes **lend oneself to**「〜に適している」 **much less**「まして〜でない」 **seemingly innocuous**「一見無害に見える」 **died tuna shavings (=dried bonito flakes)**「かつお節」 **animal-based**「動物性の」 **ideological reason**「イデオロギーに関する理由」 **by-product**「副産物」 **by no means**「決して〜ではない」

A Vocabulary

次の単語の意味を (a) 〜 (g) から選び、下線上にその記号を書きなさい。

1. aesthetically ______ (a) a food that is the main part of a diet
2. cuisine ______ (b) a person who does not eat animal products at all
3. vegan ______ (c) a process by which two things affect each other
4. liberally ______ (d) a style of cooking
5. prevalence ______ (e) generous; free
6. staple ______ (f) in a way that gives pleasure through beauty
7. interaction ______ (g) the state or condition of being very common

B True or False

(　　) 内の適切な単語を選び英文を完成しなさい。次にその英文が本文の内容に合っていれば T (True)、間違っていれば F (False) を選びなさい。

1. According to the author, most Japanese dishes are vegetarian (**friend / friendly**). **[T F]**
2. Unlike vegetarians, vegans do not eat or drink things (**like / similar**) cheese or milk. **[T F]**
3. According to the author, it is (**impossible / impossibly**) to be a vegetarian in Japan. **[T F]**

2 Conversation

A Listen and Write 21

次の会話を聞いて空所に単語を書きなさい。

M: What do you feel like having tonight?
W: Let's eat in! We [1](　　　　　) done that for a while.
M: Sure. What do you have in [2](　　　　　)?
W: Hmmm ... I'm in the [3](　　　　　) for some Chinese takeaway.
M: Great. I know a quaint little restaurant nearby. They have egg rolls that are to [4](　　　　　) for.
W: Sounds yummy. I'll get my purse.

B Listen and Choose 22

質問を聞いて空所に単語を書き、最も適切な答えを (A) 〜 (C) から選びなさい。

1. (　　　　　) will the man and woman (　　　　　) tonight?
(A) Go out for dinner.
(B) Have a takeaway dinner at home.
(C) They haven't decided.

2. (　　　　　) will the man and woman (　　　　　)(　　　　　) dinner?
(A) They will ask the restaurant to deliver their food.
(B) They will eat at a Chinese restaurant.
(C) They will go to the restaurant and pick up their food.

3 Text Completion

次の文章を読んで、空所に入れる最も適切なものを (A) ～ (C) から選びなさい。

It is now estimated that one in every 13 children has a food allergy. What is _(1)_ is that many children with food allergies are allergic to more than one kind of food. More than 170 kinds of food have been found to cause allergic reactions. The most _(2)_ are milk, eggs, peanuts, nuts, wheat, soy, fish, and shellfish. Allergic reactions to food can range from an itchy mouth to having difficulty breathing. Extreme reactions can result in anaphylactic shock, which _(3)_.

1. (A) bad
   (B) worse
   (C) worst

2. (A) common
   (B) popular
   (C) unusual

3. (A) can occur quickly and cause death
   (B) causes your mouth to itch
   (C) not as serious as most people think

4 Composition

A 日本文を参考にして (　　) 内の語句を正しく並べ替えなさい。

1. Vegetarians consume dairy products and eggs, but vegans (animals / any food / avoid / from / is derived / that).
   (菜食主義者は乳製品や卵を食べますが、完全菜食主義者は動物から得られるどんな食べ物も避けます)

2. While vegetarianism is still new to Japan, (actually some / are / meals / there / you / vegetarian friendly) can enjoy.
   (菜食主義は日本ではまだ新しいですが、あなたが楽しむことができる菜食主義者に優しい料理が実際にいくつかあります)

3. If you get the chance to try *shojin ryori*, it makes a light and healthy meal, (a fun / and / experience / cultural / for / is) a vegetarian.
   (もし精進料理を食べる機会があれば、軽い健康的な食事になり、菜食主義者にとって楽しい文化体験です)

B (　　) 内の語句を使って、質問に対する応答文を考えなさい。

1. Which do you prefer, Japanese cuisine or some other cuisine? Why?
   (used to like / fast food / I am really into / a healthy diet)

2. Many people feel that vegetarianism makes for a healthier lifestyle. Do you agree or disagree? Why or why not?
   (I am not that familiar with / vegetarian / mainly eat)

Unit 8 Paid Days Off

日本人は西洋の人々と比べると有給休暇を取ることが少なく、残業が多いと言われます。しかし、この慣習は変わりつつあります。日本とアメリカでは有給休暇に対する考え方が異なりますが、その理由は何でしょうか。

1 Reading 23

Japanese people are hard-workers. In fact, they work some of the longest hours in the world. Despite a national labor law that limits working time to 8 hours per day, it is not uncommon for employees to regularly put in 10 or even 12 hours each day. In many cases, the first 20 to 40 hours of overtime that an employee works is considered "service overtime" and is unpaid. In addition, though Japanese workers are entitled to 15 paid days off a year, most Japanese use only a small portion of their allotted paid days off. Fortunately, this practice is becoming less common. More and more Japanese are spending less time at work and more time with their families.

Other countries like the U.K., France, and Germany provide their employees with 30 days of paid time off and encourage their workers to use these days to recover and relax. The situation in the U.S. is dramatically different, however. U.S. workers are allotted 10 public holidays, though these are not guaranteed to come with pay. In fact, paid time off is left to the employer's discretion.

Over 28 million Americans do not receive any paid vacation time or paid holidays. Moreover, of those workers who do receive paid vacation time, more and more are reluctant to take time off. A recent study showed that nearly 50% of workers refused to take the paid time off they were given by employers. They cited reasons like having too much work to do, being unfavorably looked upon by their boss, being unable to afford a vacation, and even loving their job too much.

It may well be that America will soon become the country with the world's longest working hours. The question is, "Is that necessarily a good thing?"

Notes **service overtime**「サービス残業」 **in addition**「さらに」 **paid day off (=paid time off, paid vacation time)**「有給休暇」 **public holiday**「公休日」 **come with**「～を伴う」 **take time off**「休みを取る」 **may well**「おそらく～でしょう」

A Vocabulary

次の単語の意味を (a) ～ (g) から選び、下線上にその記号を書きなさい。

1. uncommon ____ (a) individual choice or judgment
2. entitle ____ (b) not ordinary; unusual; rare
3. allot ____ (c) not willing to do something
4. guarantee ____ (d) to assign as a share or portion
5. discretion ____ (e) to give someone a right
6. reluctant ____ (f) to mention something as an example
7. cite ____ (g) to promise with certainty

B True or False

(　　) 内の適切な単語を選び英文を完成しなさい。次にその英文が本文の内容に合っていれば T (True)、間違っていれば F (False) を選びなさい。

1. In Japan, it is illegal to work more (**over / than**) eight hours per day. **[T F]**
2. In the U.S., companies must give their employees 30 days of (**pay / paid**) time off. **[T F]**
3. The author feels that American workers will continue to work long hours and (**take / taking**) less time off from work. **[T F]**

2 Conversation

A Listen and Write 24

次の会話を聞いて空所に単語を書きなさい。

M: Hey, Theresa! This is Bob calling. What are you doing later tonight? Do you feel like seeing a movie?
W: I'd love to, but I was called into work. Actually, I'm just [1](　　　　　) ready.
M: You're kidding! I thought you had the day [2](　　　　　).
W: I did, but one of the [3](　　　　　) called in sick. So I have to cover her shift.
M: But you've been working for two weeks [4](　　　　　)!
W: I know, but it's overtime pay, and I need the money.

B Listen and Choose 25

質問を聞いて空所に単語を書き、最も適切な答えを (A) ～ (C) から選びなさい。

1. (　　　　)(　　　　) the man (　　　　　) the woman?
(A) He is worried that she is not feeling well.
(B) He wants her to come to work.
(C) He wants to invite her to see a movie.

2. Why was the woman (　　　　　)(　　　　) go to (　　　　　)?
(A) A co-worker is sick.
(B) It's going for her regular shift.
(C) The hospital is busy, and they need extra help.

3 Text Completion

次の文章を読んで、空所に入れる最も適切なものを (A) ～ (C) から選びなさい。

The so-called gig economy is defined as a labor market where companies offer people short-term contracts or freelance work. These people are not _(1)_ employees of the company, and the jobs are not permanent. Because of this, gig workers are not paid regular wages. Rather, they are paid only for the "gigs" (jobs) they do. Workers engaged in the gig economy enjoy the _(2)_ flexible hours, while employers benefit from not having to pay the costs associated with having permanent employees. Despite these benefits, _(3)_.

1. (A) necessarily
   (B) necessary
   (C) necessity
2. (A) advantage of
   (B) charge of
   (C) part in
3. (A) both employers and employees benefit from this arrangement
   (B) permanent employees work harder than their gig counterparts
   (C) this arrangement also has several downsides

4 Composition

A 日本文を参考にして（　　）内の語句を正しく並べ替えなさい。

1. Under Japan's labor laws, all (a minimum / are / 10 days / employees / guaranteed / of) paid leave per year.
   （日本の労働法の下で、すべての社員は 1 年に最低 10 日の有給休暇が保障されています）

   ____

2. Japan has a lot of national holidays, and these holidays (factors / have become / important / in / the Japanese / the way) take paid days off.
   （日本にはたくさんの国民の祝日があり、これらの休暇が日本人の有給休暇の取り方において重要な要因になっています）

   ____

3. Many Japanese workers don't take (fear of / for / their annual / leave entitlement / inconveniencing / their) colleagues.
   （多くの日本の労働者は同僚に迷惑をかけないように、年次休暇の資格を行使しません）

   ____

B （　　）内の語句を使って、質問に対する応答文を考えなさい。

1. Do you think Japanese people work too hard or too much? Why or why not?
   (spend too much time / with their families)

   ____

2. Which is more attractive to you, a job with a great salary but long hours, or a job with an average salary but where you can spend more time with your friends and family? Explain.
   (I would prefer having / rather than / create a strong bond)

   ____

Unit 9 Greetings

挨拶の仕方は文化によって異なります。宗教やパーソナルスペース、ジェンダーによって決まることもあります。特に外国の人と交流するときは、お互いにそれぞれの挨拶方法を理解することが大切です。

1 Reading 26

Greetings around the world vary from culture to culture. The way people greet each other is often determined by cultural customs and beliefs such as religion, the appropriate amount of personal space, and gender roles. In Japan, as well as in other parts of Asia, greeting by bowing is the norm. People in Thailand greet each other with a *wai*, pressing their palms together and bowing slightly. The height of the hands and the depth of the bow depend on the age and social status of the person being greeted, and communicate the greeter's respect for him or her.

Gender can also influence how people greet each other. In many Muslim countries, there is a strict code of interaction between men and women. Social interactions between non-related members of the opposite sex are frowned upon. For example, if you are a man, shaking hands with a Muslim woman is not allowed. Other countries have a much more *laissez-faire* attitude. Greetings in many Latin American countries, for example, are much more physical. In places like Argentina, Chile, and Brazil, it is not uncommon to be greeted warmly by both men and women with several kisses on the cheek!

Some countries have very distinct greeting practices. The Maori *Hongi* greeting involves two people pressing their noses together. The Inuit, a people in northern Canada, greet each other with a *kunik* – pressing your nose and mouth on someone's forehead or cheek and then breathing on that person. Because there are so many different ways of greeting, when you travel you can avoid embarrassing and awkward social interactions by knowing and respecting these differences.

Notes **personal space**「パーソナルスペース」 **Muslim country**「イスラム教の国」 **strict code**「厳格な決まり」 **social interaction**「社会的交流」 **frown upon**「眉をひそめる」 ***laissez-faire* attitude**「自由放任的な態度」 **not uncommon**「珍しくない」 **the Maori**「マオリ族」ニュージーランドの先住民 **the Inuit**「イヌイット族」

A Vocabulary

次の単語の意味を (a) ～ (g) から選び、下線上にその記号を書きなさい。

1. vary	_____	(a) a standard level or custom
2. appropriate	_____	(b) right or suited for some purpose
3. norm	_____	(c) the inside part of the hand
4. palm	_____	(d) the position or rank of a person in society
5. status	_____	(e) uncomfortable; shameful
6. avoid	_____	(f) to be different; differ
7. embarrassing	_____	(g) to stay away from something

B True or False

(　　) 内の適切な単語を選び英文を完成しなさい。次にその英文が本文の内容に合っていれば T (True)、間違っていれば F (False) を選びなさい。

1. Cultural customs and beliefs determine how people (**greet / greets**) each other. **[T F]**

2. In some countries, it is rude for a man to shake hands (**to / with**) a woman he has just met. **[T F]**

3. The author believes that understanding the different ways people greet each other (**are / is**) not important or necessary. **[T F]**

2 Conversation

A Listen and Write 27

次の会話を聞いて空所に単語を書きなさい。

W: You must be the new hire. My name's Kathryn, but everyone here [1](　　　　　) me Kate.

M: Hi, Kate. I'm Geoff. Nice to [2](　　　　　) you.

W: Likewise. Dan has told me a lot about you.

M: Really? I hope he said good [3](　　　　　).

W: Of course he did! I'm looking forward to working with you. Let me [4](　　　　　) you around the office.

M: That would be great!

B Listen and Choose 28

質問を聞いて空所に単語を書き、最も適切な答えを (A) ～ (C) から選びなさい。

1. What is the (　　　　　)(　　　　　　　　　) name?

(A) Dan.　　(B) Geoff.　　(C) Kate.

2. Which of these phrases has a (　　　　　　　)(　　　　　　　) to "Likewise"?

(A) Me, too.　　(B) Of course.　　(C) That would be great.

3 Text Completion

次の文章を読んで、空所に入れる最も適切な語句や文を (A) 〜 (C) から選びなさい。

Your first day on the job is crucial because it sets the tone for how your co-workers will see you. It is important _(1)_ a good first impression. Find out what kind of dress code is appropriate for your workplace. You don't want to _(2)_. Plan your commute ahead of time. Arriving at work too early can be as bad as arriving late. Lastly, keep an open mind. _(3)_

1. (A) making
   (B) for make
   (C) to make

2. (A) stand by
   (B) stand out
   (C) stand up

3. (A) Be prepared for class.
   (B) Don't trust anyone.
   (C) Follow your heart.

4 Composition

A 日本文を参考にして (　　) 内の語句を正しく並べ替えなさい。ただし文頭に来る語も小文字にしてある。

1. (important / is / it / the proper / to learn / way) to shake hands, because making a good first impression is essential in many social situations.
   (良い第一印象を与えることが多くの社会状況において必要なので、握手をする適切な方法を学ぶことは大切です)

   ____

2. If you grasp someone's hand too firmly, you'll give the impression of being aggressive. However, shaking someone's hand too (a sign of / and lack / as / is viewed / limply / weakness) of confidence.
   (あまりきつく人の手を握ると、攻撃的な印象を与えます。しかし、あまりゆるく握手をすると、弱さや自信のなさの表れと見られます)

   ____

3. Whether you're shaking hands with a friend or client, always (eye contact / interested / maintain / that / to show / you're) in that person.
   (友だちであろうと顧客であろうと、握手をしているときは、その人に関心があることを示すために、いつもアイコンタクトをしておいてください)

   ____

B (　　) 内の語句を使って、質問に対する応答文を考えなさい。

1. Practice greeting your classmates using a handshake. Does it feel different from traditional Japanese greetings? How?
   (my teacher asks / practice / For me, shaking hands feels)

   ____

2. Some people say that children these days do not care as much about making proper greetings as they used to. Do you agree or disagree? Why?
   (Nowadays, it seems that / bowing and saying)

   ____

Unit 10 Napping in Public

日本では電車やバスの中で居眠りをする人をよく見かけます。ごく普通の光景ですが、外国の人にはおかしく、奇妙に見えます。人前で居眠りをするのは、日本が安全な国である証なのでしょうか。

1 Reading 29

Japanese people are notorious for their long hours, whether they are working 10-hour days and attending company drinking parties after work, or studying at school all day and then going to a cram school for another three hours afterwards. Thus, it is not surprising that so many Japanese people are tired – and even less surprising that they take advantage of every opportunity to "catch a few z's."

Napping in Japan is something of an art form. There is even a separate word, *inemuri* (sleeping while present), that distinguishes a unique kind of napping from regular napping, *hirune.* Of course it is not uncommon in other countries to take time out for naps. But the place for napping is usually somewhere private and out of sight. In most other countries, public napping is sure to draw some ridicule and may even make the napper vulnerable to being robbed.

In Japan, however, we can find people of all ages and all walks of life soundly sleeping in parks and libraries, and on trains. Because Japan is a relatively safe country and no one worries that they will wake up missing their wallet or purse, people feel little apprehension about falling asleep next to strangers. Moreover, because everyone recognizes that hard work is the reason behind these naps, most Japanese are quite tolerant of this behavior.

Foreigners visiting Japan will often look at nappers with some amusement and fascination, as it is not something that the visitors would even consider doing in their own country. Many foreigners are amazed that not only is it possible for people to nap safely in public, but also that they are able to sleep so soundly despite the commotion around them.

Notes **in public**「人前で」 **cram school**「予備校、塾」 **even less**「まして〜でない」 **take advantage of**「〜を利用する」 **catch a few z's**「居眠りをする」 **something of**「ちょっとした」 **while present**「座ったままで」 **take time out for**「〜の時間を取る」 **out of sight**「人目に触れない」 **all walks of life**「あらゆる職業・地位」

A Vocabulary

次の単語の意味を (a) ～ (g) から選び、下線上にその記号を書きなさい。

1. vulnerable ____ (a) an anxious feeling that something bad will happen
2. distinguish ____ (b) being in danger or at risk of
3. ridicule ____ (c) completely or deeply
4. apprehension ____ (d) noisy disturbance
5. tolerant ____ (e) the act of making fun of something
6. soundly ____ (f) willing to accept others' feelings, habits, or beliefs
7. commotion ____ (g) to recognize differences between things

B True or False

(　　) 内の適切な単語を選び英文を完成しなさい。次にその英文が本文の内容に合っていれば T (True)、間違っていれば F (False) を選びなさい。

1. Japanese spend a lot of (**time / times**) working or studying. **[T F]**

2. One reason (**gives / given**) for why Japanese can sleep in public is that Japan is safer than many other countries. **[T F]**

3. Foreigners are often (**surprising / surprised**) that people can sleep on trains, despite there being so much noise around them. **[T F]**

2 Conversation

A Listen and Write 30

次の会話を聞いて空所に単語を書きなさい。

M: What a day! I'm beat.
W: Do you still want to [1](　　　　) us for some drinks after work?
M: I don't know. I just feel like going home and [2](　　　　　　) on the couch.
W: Come on. Everyone's been looking forward to this all [3](　　　　).
M: Well, I suppose it'll be good to [4](　　　　) down with some friends.
W: Great! I'll get your coat.

B Listen and Choose 31

質問を聞いて空所に単語を書き、最も適切な答えを (A) ～ (C) から選びなさい。

1. (　　　　)(　　　　　) the man (　　　　　)?
(A) Angry. (B) Happy. (C) Tired.

2. (　　　　　)(　　　　) the man probably (　　　　) after work?
(A) Go home.
(B) Have a drink with his co-workers.
(C) Sleep on the couch.

3 Text Completion

次の文章を読んで、空所に入れる最も適切な語句や文を (A) 〜 (C) から選びなさい。

Everyone understands that sleep is an important part of our lives. We spend a third of our lives _(1)_. Sleeping is also necessary for good health, yet few of us make sleep a priority. Most people go through the day with a "sleep debt" and _(2)_ what being "really rested" feels like. Moreover, many people drink stimulants like coffee and energy drinks to keep themselves awake and alert. They also work under artificial lighting and use a variety of digital devices, all of which interfere with the body's natural "circadian rhythm". _(3)_

1. (A) asleep
   (B) for sleeping
   (C) sleep
2. (A) are forgotten
   (B) have forgotten
   (C) have been forgetting
3. (A) All of these habits make getting to sleep much more difficult.
   (B) People should take a nap if they feel tired or sleepy.
   (C) Sleeping is difficult for people who have busy schedules.

4 Composition

A 日本文を参考にして (　　) 内の語句を正しく並べ替えなさい。

1. Foreigners may feel a little (in / Japanese people / napping / see / surprised / to) public.
   (外国の人は、日本人が人前で居眠りをしているのを見て、少し驚くかもしれません)

   ____

2. Japanese people are often tired when (a nap / and / from / returning / take / work or school) on the train.
   (日本人は仕事や学校から帰るとき、しばしば疲れて電車の中で居眠りをします)

   ____

3. This is surely because Japan is a safe country, (be / not / pickpocketed / where / will / you) on the train even if you are fast asleep.
   (これはきっと日本が、ぐっすり居眠りしていても、電車の中でスリに遭わない安全な国だからです)

   ____

B (　　) 内の語句を使って、質問に対する応答文を考えなさい。

1. Have you ever fallen asleep in public? What happened?
   (Once [A while ago] / I fell asleep / missed my stop)

   ____

2. Visitors to Japan often comment on how safe Japan is. Do you agree or disagree? Why?
   (Compared to / I believe / safe)

   ____

Unit 11 Parenting Styles

外国の人は、日本では子どもだけで学校や公園に行く様子を見て驚きます。これは安全な環境や地域の共同責任によるものでしょうか。日米の子育ての違いについて考えてみましょう。

1 Reading 32

It is quite common in Japan to see very young children walking to and from schools or parks. Foreigners here are often surprised by how responsible such young children seem. Visitors to Japan note that young Japanese children generally display more mature behavior and better self-sufficiency, and are substantially less fussy than their peers in other countries. Many factors help explain this, including a safer environment and greater emphasis on communal responsibility.

When it comes to how children are raised, one characteristic difference between Japan and places like the U.S. and Canada has to do with parenting style. In general, there are two kinds of parenting styles: *proximal* and *distal.* Proximal parenting involves consistent, prolonged contact between parent and child, while distal parenting emphasizes eye contact and communication through facial expressions and gestures. Japanese parents typically engage in the former, which means that it is not unusual for parents and children to sleep, bathe, and play together.

Japanese mothers spend a lot of time with their children during the first two years of a child's life. Most spend only 2 hours a week away from their children, whereas mothers in America average 24 hours a week away from them. Unlike American parents, Japanese moms and dads do not regularly employ babysitters or engage in "date nights" or parent getaways. Because Japanese mothers spend so much time with their children, alleviating fuss is a priority. As a result, Japanese parents, particularly mothers, are adept at anticipating their children's needs as well as at helping children who feel upset control their emotions, a practice known as self-regulation.

Though many Westerners might be quick to judge these practices as coddling or even spoiling children, it is obvious that this kind of parenting produces significant benefits for children's behavior – and for society.

Notes **parenting style**「子育てスタイル」 **self-sufficiency**「自立心」 **communal responsibility**「共同責任」 **have to do with**「〜と関係がある」 **engage in**「〜に携わる」 **date night**「夜のデート」 **parent getaway**「親の息抜きの外出」 **be adept at**「〜が上手である」 **self-regulation**「自己規制」

A Vocabulary

次の単語の意味を (a) 〜 (g) から選び、下線上にその記号を書きなさい。

1. priority ____ (a) a thing that is more important than another
2. mature ____ (b) an advantage gained from something
3. substantially ____ (c) considerably; to a large extent
4. babysitter ____ (d) showing the mental qualities of an adult
5. alleviate ____ (e) someone who takes care of babies
6. coddle ____ (f) to reduce trouble; lessen
7. benefit ____ (g) to treat kids with too much care; indulge

B True or False

(　　) 内の適切な単語を選び英文を完成しなさい。次にその英文が本文の内容に合っていれば T (True)、間違っていれば F (False) を選びなさい。

1. Visitors to Japan are often (**surprising / surprised**) by how unruly Japanese children are. **[T F]**

2. American parents spend (**much / more**) time with their young children than do Japanese parents. **[T F]**

3. Some parents in the West feel that Japanese parents (**spoil / spoiling**) their children too much. **[T F]**

2 Conversation

A Listen and Write 33

次の会話を聞いて空所に単語を書きなさい。

W: Turn off the video game, George. It's time to do your homework.
M: Just five more [1](　　　　　　　).
W: I said, "Turn it off now and do your homework!"
M: But I am already finished, and I'm about to go past this [2](　　　　　　).
W: Finished? Really? [3](　　　　　　) playing that game now and finish your homework or you won't be able to play any videos for the [4](　　　　　　) of the week.
M: Okay. Okay. But you're no fun.
W: I'm your mother. It's my job not to be fun.

B Listen and Choose 34

質問を聞いて空所に単語を書き、最も適切な答えを (A) 〜 (C) から選びなさい。

1. What will (　　　　　　　) if George does not (　　　　)(　　　　) do his homework?
(A) He will be allowed to play the game longer.
(B) He will not be able to play video games for a week.
(C) He will have to go to bed early.

2. What will George probably (　　　　)(　　　　　)?
(A) He will continue playing the video game and do his homework later.
(B) He will go to school and finish his homework.
(C) He will turn off the video game and do his homework.

3 Text Completion

次の文章を読んで、空所に入れる最も適切な語や文を (A) ～ (C) から選びなさい。

The Marshmallow Experiment was an experiment carried out by the psychologist Walter Mischel in the 1960s and 1970s. He wanted to examine when people's ability to control themselves and _(1)_ wait for something they want begins in children. In this experiment, he gave young children the choice of receiving a reward (a marshmallow) right now, _(2)_ to wait and receive two marshmallows about 15 minutes later. What he found was that children who could control themselves and wait longer had better life outcomes. _(3)_

1. (A) patience
   (B) patient
   (C) patiently

2. (A) but
   (B) or
   (C) while

3. (A) They did better at school, had better jobs, and were generally happier people.
   (B) They enjoyed eating their marshmallows more than those who could not wait.
   (C) They would always struggle at school and have difficulties in their workplace.

4 Composition

A 日本文を参考にして (　　) 内の語句を正しく並べ替えなさい。ただし文頭に来る語も小文字にしてある。

1. Parenting styles differ according to the region, and are (and the people / by / of / influenced / that area / the culture) who live there.
   (子育てスタイルは地域によって異なり、その地域の文化と、そこに住んでいる人々に影響を受けます)

   ____

2. Western mothers start (encourage / in / influencing / that / their children / ways) independence, which is why many feel that the Japanese parenting style spoils children.
   (西洋の母親は、独立心を促進するような方法で子どもに影響を与え始めます。そういうわけで多くの人は、日本人の子育てスタイルは、子どもを甘やかしていると感じています)

   ____

3. (children / good parenting / is / raising / of / the goal) who can become contributing members of society.
   (良い子育ての目標は、社会に貢献する一員になれる子どもを育てることです)

   ____

B (　　) 内の語句を使って、質問に対する応答文を考えなさい。

1. Do you think Japanese parents coddle their young children? Why?
   (These days, I believe that / For example, / whatever)

   ____

2. Some people say that some parents give their children too much freedom. Do you agree or disagree? Why?
   (In fact, in my experience / enough freedom / after school activities)

   ____

Unit 12 Gender Segregation

性別職務分離とは、性別により異なる職務につかされることを指します。諸外国と比べて、日本では女性管理職者が少ないと言われますが、女性は現状に満足しているのでしょうか。

1 Reading 35

When we talk about gender segregation, we may not immediately think about the situation in advanced, industrialized countries, much less Japan. However, in a recent report released by the World Economic Forum, Japan was ranked 110th in the world, far below countries like the U.S. (51st), Canada (16th), and the U.K. (15th). By region, of the 18 countries in East Asia and the Pacific, Japan ranks 16th, coming behind such countries as Australia, New Zealand, and the Philippines.

One area of disparity is management positions. In Japan, although women make up 43% of the workforce, they only account for 13% of management positions. Compare this with the U.S., where 43% of managers are women, or the Philippines, where 49% of managers are female. The main reason for this difference is the persistence of traditional gender roles in Japan. Unlike in Western countries, where many women pursue high-end careers in professions like engineering, law, and research, women in Japan tend to be underrepresented in these fields. Among OECD countries, Japan has the lowest proportion of women to men in these professions.

Moreover, in places like the U.S., family responsibilities are equally shared between husband and wife, but in Japan these responsibilities fall almost exclusively to women, making balancing career and family more difficult. Additionally, when women in Japan join companies, they are often expected to quit at a certain age when they get married and accept their role as stay-at-home mothers.

Interestingly, Japanese women do not seem to see this as too much of a problem, mainly because they enjoy a high rate of education and employment in safer and more stable jobs. In fact, in a recent survey, Japanese women reported that they are not necessarily looking to secure more advanced positions, being satisfied in their current roles.

Notes **much less**「ましてや〜でない」 **World Economic Forum**「世界経済フォーラム」 **management position**「管理職」 **high-end career**「最高のキャリア」 **OECD** (=Organization for Economic Cooperation and Development)「経済協力開発機構」 **fall almost exclusively to**「ほぼもっぱら〜の役目になる」 **stay-at-home mother**「専業主婦」 **be looking to**「〜しようと思っている」

A Vocabulary

次の単語の意味を (a) 〜 (g) から選び、下線上にその記号を書きなさい。

1. release ____ (a) a part of the world; area
2. region ____ (b) a job that requires special skills and education
3. workforce ____ (c) the attitude of someone who continues to do something
4. persistence ____ (d) the number of people who work or are available for work
5. pursue ____ (e) to make something available to the public
6. profession ____ (f) to state as being lower than is actually the case
7. underrepresent ____ (g) to try to achieve something

B True or False

(　　) 内の適切な語句を選び英文を完成しなさい。次にその英文が本文の内容に合っていれば T (True)、間違っていれば F (False) を選びなさい。

1. Gender segregation is not a problem that affects (**industrialize / industrialized**) nations. **[T F]**

2. More women in (**Philippine / the Philippines**) are managers than women in Japan are. **[T F]**

3. Japanese women generally do not seem to be (**bother / bothered**) by gender segregation in the workforce. **[T F]**

2 Conversation

A Listen and Write 36

次の会話を聞いて空所に単語を書きなさい。

M: Congratulations! I heard that you are up for a promotion.
W: That's right. There is a marketing position [1](　　　　　) up at the head office.
M: Well, they will be lucky to have you, but we are going to [2](　　　　　) you here.
W: Not so fast. They haven't decided yet. They'll make their final [3](　　　　　) at the end of the fiscal year.
M: I don't think you have to [4](　　　　　).
W: Regardless, I'll just continue to do what I do and keep my fingers crossed.

B Listen and Choose 37

質問を聞いて空所に単語を書き、最も適切な答えを (A) 〜 (C) から選びなさい。

1. (　　　　) does the man (　　　　　　　　　　) the woman?
(A) She has a new baby.
(B) She is being considered for a higher position.
(C) She received a big bonus.

2. When will the woman (　　　　) whether or not (　　　　)(　　　　　　) the promotion?
(A) Around the end of March, when the fiscal year ends.
(B) At the end of the current month.
(C) In two weeks, after the new year begins.

3 Text Completion

次の図表を見て、空所に入れる最も適切な語句を (A) ～ (C) から選びなさい。

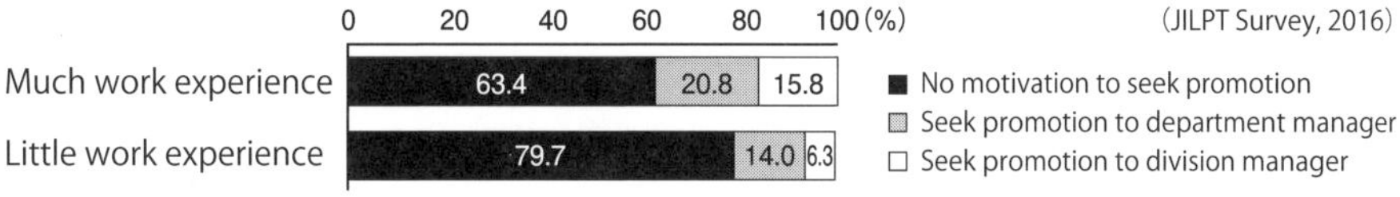

1. _(1)_ of women with "Much work experience" are interested in upper management positions.
   (A) A little under one-fifth (B) A little over one-third (C) Almost two-thirds
2. _(2)_ with "Little work experience" are happy in their current position.
   (A) Under 1 in 10 women (B) Over 6 in 10 women (C) Almost 8 in 10 women
3. In total, approximately _(3)_ of women are satisfied in their current position.
   (A) 33% (B) 65% (C) 72%

4 Composition

A 日本文を参考にして (　　) 内の語句を正しく並べ替えなさい。ただし文頭に来る語も小文字にしてある。

1. In Japan, (are / attributed / female managers / of / the low numbers / to) the fact that many female employees choose not to be promoted, or they leave their job at an early age.
   (日本で女性の管理職者数が少ないのは、多くの女性社員は昇進しないことを選ぶか、若い頃に仕事を辞めるという事実が原因です)

   ____

2. (family / a management position / combining / responsibilities / seems / with having) to be difficult for Japanese women to carry off.
   (管理職と家族の責任を両立することは、日本女性にとって、やりとげるのが難しいように思えます)

   ____

3. Japanese companies' (a source / insistence / is / long / on / work hours) of gender inequality when it comes to the attainment of managerial positions.
   (管理職を得ることになると、日本の企業が、長い労働時間を求めることが男女不平等の源です)

   ____

B (　　) 内の語句を使って、質問に対する応答文を考えなさい。

1. Do you think men and women are treated equally in the Japanese workforce? Why or why not?
   (gender equality / major concern / important issue / field of technology)

   ____

2. Fewer and fewer Japanese couples are interested in starting a family. Why do you think that is?
   (I feel most Japanese couples / make ends meet / cost of living)

   ____

Unit 13 Japanese Hospitality

日本の顧客サービスは優れていると言われますが、なぜでしょうか。日本と世界の他の国々における消費者の態度が違うからかもしれません。ひどいサービスに対する消費者の反応について考えてみましょう。

1 Reading 38

Japan is renowned for its great sense of hospitality and outstanding service culture. That is not to say that hospitality is lacking in Western culture. The Western expression “The customer is always right” is not all that different from the Japanese saying, “The customer is god.” Furthermore, many service industries in the West place large importance on customer perception. Part of that has to do with ensuring that customers are treated with respect. So, why does Japan excel at customer service? One important reason may well be in the difference between Japanese consumers and those in the rest of the world.

A while ago, a survey was conducted asking consumers from different countries how willing they were to take their business someplace else after they had experienced poor customer service. The result was surprising. Of the nine countries sampled, Japanese consumers ranked the least forgiving. Over 50% of Japanese consumers polled responded that even after only one experience of poor customer service, they would spend their money at a different place.

In many Western countries, consumers tend to complain to the shop or restaurant about poor service and, in the hope for improvement, return to it. If nothing improves, Western consumers may just resign themselves to their poor experience at a particular place. Japanese, on the other hand, would rather forgo the offending business and switch to a competitor right away. Because of the large number of alternatives available to consumers in Japan, this high level of expectation raises the bar for customer service, not just for individual businesses but for industries as a whole. The result is that service industries such as retail or dining out maintain high levels of customer service, making poor customer service the exception rather than the norm.

Notes **be renowned for**「〜で名高い」 **that is not to say that**「だからといって〜と言っているのではない」 **not all that**「それほど〜でない」 **have to do with**「〜に関連する」 **excel at**「〜に優れている」 **may well be**「たぶん〜だろう」 **a while ago**「少し前に」 **the least forgiving**「最も寛大でない」 **on the other hand**「一方」 **would rather**「どちらかというと〜する方が良いと考える」

A Vocabulary

次の単語の意味を (a) ～ (g) から選び、下線上にその記号を書きなさい。

1. outstanding _____ (a) a choice among more than two things
2. treat _____ (b) a feeling of admiration; reverence
3. respect _____ (c) extremely good or excellent
4. conduct _____ (d) to ask a question in order to get information
5. poll _____ (e) to deal with something in a particular way
6. forgo _____ (f) to give up the use of something
7. alternative _____ (g) to plan and do something

B True or False

(　　) 内の適切な単語を選び英文を完成しなさい。次にその英文が本文の内容に合っていれば T (True)、間違っていれば F (False) を選びなさい。

1. The idea that "the customer is god" is (**unique / uniquely**) Japanese and is never found in the West. **[T F]**

2. Japanese consumers are generally more (**forgiven / forgiving**) of poor customer service than Western consumers. **[T F]**

3. Many shoppers in the U.S. will continue to (**shop / shopping**) at the same store even if they have had poor customer service there. **[T F]**

2 Conversation

A Listen and Write 39

次の会話を聞いて空所に単語を書きなさい。

M: How was your date last night?
W: Don't ask! It was probably the [1](　　　　　　) experience of my life!
M: Why? What happened?
W: Well, everything seemed okay until [2](　　　　　　). Then, my date started coughing and choking. Apparently, he had an allergic reaction to one of the [3](　　　　　　) we had eaten. The restaurant called an ambulance, and I spent the rest of the evening with him at the hospital.
M: Wow! That is [4](　　　　　　). So, will you see him again?
W: Ha ha. He was cute, so probably, but no more dinner dates!

B Listen and Choose 40

質問を聞いて空所に単語を書き、最も適切な答えを (A) ～ (C) から選びなさい。

1. What (　　　　　　　　)(　　　) the woman's date at the restaurant?
(A) He arrived late.
(B) He drank too much.
(C) He had an allergic reaction to a food.

2. What did the woman (　　　)(　　　　　) dinner?
(A) She went home.
(B) She went to another restaurant.
(C) She went with her date to the hospital.

3 Text Completion

次の文章を読んで、空所に入れる最も適切な語句や文を (A) ～ (C) から選びなさい。

With so many competitors, offering good service is essential for a business to survive. Business owners understand that even one bad customer-service experience can _(1)_ a customer permanently. Moreover, in the age of social networking, even one instance of poor customer service can have wide ramifications. _(2)_ this, many companies invest a lot of time and money training their employees.

1. (A) acquire (B) lose (C) promise
2. (A) Because of (B) In order to (C) Despite
3. According to the following table, in which country would customers be least likely to spend their money elsewhere after an experience of poor customer service?
   (A) Canada (B) Hong Kong (C) the U.K.

Country	Percentage
Canada	32
Hong Kong	23
the U.K.	37

Percentage of customers who would take their business to a competitor after poor customer service

(Japan Today Survey, 2017)

4 Composition

A 日本文を参考にして (　　) 内の語句を正しく並べ替えなさい。ただし文頭に来る語も小文字にしてある。

1. (astonished / by / every visitor / is / its high / to Japan) level of customer service, which usually exceeds customers' expectations.
   (日本に来る訪問者はみんな、たいてい顧客の期待を超える高いレベルの顧客サービスに驚きます)

   ____

2. The Japanese spirit of service is called *Omotenashi*, (a mindset / between / is / that makes / the relationship / which) customer and seller a long-lasting one.
   (日本人のサービス精神は「おもてなし」と呼ばれ、顧客と売り手の間の関係を長く続くものにする考え方です)

   ____

3. Japanese hospitality is exemplified (pride and effort / by / in / to / visitors / welcoming) one's place of business.
   (日本人のおもてなしは、訪問者をビジネスの場に歓迎する際の誇りと努力で示されます)

   ____

B (　　) 内の語句を使って、質問に対する応答文を考えなさい。

1. Have you ever experienced "poor" customer service? If so, what happened?
   (Once, while I was / I noticed)

   ____

2. Some people say that some Japanese companies do a lot to take care of the customer but don't take very good care of their own employees. Do you agree or disagree? Why?
   (partly true / not only ... but also / work long hours)

   ____

Unit 14 Tax

消費税は国によって違います。西洋の多くの国では消費税を商品の価格に含めることで購入を容易にしています。カナダでは2種類の消費税があり、購入する商品によって異なります。

1 Reading 41

Popping into a convenience store in Japan and buying a soda might seem like one of the easiest things you can do. You examine your choices, choose your soda – maybe based on personal preference or on price – bring your purchase to the checkout counter, and pay the cashier for the item. No matter which product you buy, you have to pay the consumption tax, which has been nationally set at 8 or 10%.

Around the world, consumption tax – also called goods and services tax (GST), value added tax (VAT), or simply sales tax – can vary depending on where you are. Figuring out how much you will pay for an item can be confusing. Fortunately, many countries in Europe have made the process of buying things easier by including the VAT in the price of goods. The price you see listed for an item is exactly what you will pay for it.

In Canada, there are generally two kinds of sales tax: the Goods and Services Tax (GST), which is set by the government of Canada and applies nationally, and a Provincial Sales Tax (PST), which is determined by each province. To make things simpler, the Canadian government has introduced a Harmonized Sales Tax (HST), which is a combination of both.

When buying goods in Canada, you can expect to pay anywhere between 5 to 15% more than the listed price, depending on where you shop. To make matters more complicated, the amount of tax can vary depending on what kind of product you are buying. Residents of border towns who live between two differently taxed areas often take advantage of this and drive to and shop in different cities where lower taxes make items cheaper.

Notes **pop into**「～に立ち寄る」 **consumption tax (=sales tax)**「消費税」 **GST**「物品サービス税」 **VAT**「付加価値税」 **figure out**「～を理解する」 **PST**「州売上税」 **HST**「統合売上税」GSTとPSTを合わせた売上税 **listed price**「表示価格」 **make ... more complicated**「～をより複雑にする」 **take advantage of**「～を利用する」

A Vocabulary

次の単語の意味を (a) ～ (g) から選び、下線上にその記号を書きなさい。

1. preference ____ (a) a feeling of special liking or wanting
2. purchase ____ (b) an item that is bought
3. confuse ____ (c) political division; state; prefecture of a country
4. province ____ (d) someone who lives in a particular place
5. introduce ____ (e) to make something difficult to understand
6. combination ____ (f) to make something used or available for the first time
7. resident ____ (g) two things joined together to form a single unit

B True or False

(　　) 内の適切な語句を選び英文を完成しなさい。次にその英文が本文の内容に合っていれば T (True)、間違っていれば F (False) を選びなさい。

1. In Japan, the consumption tax of (**same / the same**) product does not vary from prefecture to prefecture. **[T F]**

2. Like Japan, (**country / countries**) in Europe do not include sales tax in the price of an item. **[T F]**

3. Some people in Canada take advantage (**for / of**) different tax rates in different areas by shopping in cities where taxes are lower. **[T F]**

2 Conversation

A Listen and Write 42

次の会話を聞いて空所に単語を書きなさい。

M: Excuse me. How much is this cell phone?
W: It's [1](　　　　　　) plus tax.
M: Okay. How much is this other one?
W: That's the newer model. It is [2](　　　　　　) plus tax, but you can also get a [3](　　　　　　) reimbursement.
M: Oh, really? Well then, I'll take the new one.
W: Great. How will you be [4](　　　　　　)?

B Listen and Choose 43

質問を聞いて空所に単語を書き、最も適切な答えを (A) ～ (C) から選びなさい。

1. What is the most likely (　　　　　　) the man (　　　　　　) the newer model?
(A) It is more expensive than the old phone.
(B) It is much cheaper than the old phone.
(C) It is the same price as the old phone.

2. How will the man probably (　　　　　　) the woman's (　　　　　　)?
(A) Do you accept credit cards?
(B) No, thank you.
(C) Only one, please.

3 Text Completion

次の文章を読んで、空所に入れる最も適切な語句や文を (A) ～ (C) から選びなさい。

Although _(1)_ likes to pay taxes, it is important to understand that taxes are an important part of helping a country run smoothly. Taxes such as sales tax and income tax are _(2)_ that governments can transfer money from the private sector to the public sector. This money can then be used to fund social projects and initiatives like healthcare and road improvements. _(3)_

1. (A) anyone
   (B) no one
   (C) someone

2. (A) few ways
   (B) its way
   (C) one way

3. (A) Tax money also goes toward the salaries of public employees such as police, firefighters, and teachers.
   (B) It is difficult to calculate exactly how much tax you will have to pay.
   (C) For this reason, we all have to pay more taxes.

4 Composition

A 日本文を参考にして (　　) 内の語句を正しく並べ替えなさい。

1. Consumption taxes are applied to the purchase of goods and services. There are (consumption taxes / depending / different / kinds of / on / the country).
   (消費税は商品やサービスを購入したときに適用されます。国によって違う種類の消費税があります)

   ____

2. In the U.S., (a consumption tax / imposed / of / on / sale / the final) a product or service is called sales tax.
   (アメリカでは、商品やサービスの最終売り上げに課せられる消費税は売上税と呼ばれます)

   ____

3. Value added tax (VAT) is a consumption tax placed (a product / at each / from / on / production / stage,) to sale. It is most commonly found in the European Union.
   (付加価値税は生産から販売まで、それぞれの段階で製品に課せられる消費税です。それはEUで最も一般的に見られます)

   ____

B (　　) 内の語句を使って、質問に対する応答文を考えなさい。

1. How often do you go shopping? What kinds of things do you like to shop for?
   (seldom [often, sometimes, rarely] / outlet malls / clearance sales)

   ____

2. Some people suggest that the government should increase the consumption tax on non-essential luxury items such as tobacco and alcohol and decrease the tax on essential items like food and medicine. Do you agree? Why or why not?
   (If the tax on cigarettes / (then) the price of smoking would / quit)

   ____

Unit 15 Returns

日本では、どこにでもショッピングセンターがあり、様々な商品を販売しています。しかし、購入した商品が気に入らなかったらどうしますか。商品を交換したり、返金してもらったりすることができるアメリカの制度を見てみましょう。

1 Reading 44

Japan is a paradise for shoppers. Wherever you go in Japan, you can find massive shopping malls that offer a huge variety of goods ranging from electronics and everyday household items to high-end luxury goods. There is also a healthy market for niche items and specialty stores. Many train stations are like mini, well-stocked shopping malls. The range of products, outstanding customer service, and competitive pricing make Japan a shopaholic's dream-come-true. But what happens when something that you buy doesn't meet your expectations?

Unlike in many countries, Japanese stores will generally not accept items for return or refund. In America, for example, returning items is a commonplace occurrence. Although there is no government policy for refunds and returns, it is general practice for stores to provide shoppers with at least 14 days to decide whether they want to keep their purchased items, during which time buyers can freely bring back unwanted goods.

It is estimated that 75% of Americans have returned an item to a retailer because the item didn't fit, or didn't meet their expectations, or just because the shoppers decided they didn't like it. This practice is so prevalent that there is even a National Returns Day, during which an estimated 1.5 million items are returned.

Big sales events like Black Friday and Boxing Day, combined with the ease of online shopping, means that more and more people can buy more and more goods. Many of these items are given as presents to friends and family, who don't necessarily need or even like these presents and choose to return them for refunds or exchanges. Unfortunately, though the system is beneficial for consumers, businesses often must carry the burden for reshipping and restocking these returned items.

Notes **household item**「家庭用品」 **niche item**「ニッチ商品」 **specialty store**「専門店」 **competitive pricing**「競合価格設定」 **shopaholic's dream-come-true**「買い物好きな人の夢を実現」 **meet one's expectation**「期待に沿う」 **National Returns Day**「ナショナルリターンズデー」返品デー **Black Friday**「ブラックフライデー」感謝祭の翌日のセール **Boxing Day**「ボクシングデー」クリスマスの翌日のセール

A Vocabulary

次の単語の意味を (a) ～ (g) から選び、下線上にその記号を書きなさい。

1. massive ＿＿＿ (a) a person or shop that sells things to customers
2. refund ＿＿＿ (b) appearing in many places; ordinary
3. commonplace ＿＿＿ (c) money that a business gives back to a customer
4. retailer ＿＿＿ (d) producing good results or effects
5. estimate ＿＿＿ (e) very large
6. beneficial ＿＿＿ (f) to give an idea or guess about the cost of something
7. restock ＿＿＿ (g) to replace goods that have been sold

B True or False

(　　) 内の適切な単語を選び英文を完成しなさい。次にその英文が本文の内容に合っていれば T (True)、間違っていれば F (False) を選びなさい。

1. Shoppers in Japan are disappointed to find that there are almost no (**specially / specialty**) stores for them to shop in. **[T F]**

2. Shoppers in America (**who / whom**) don't like what they buy often return the item to the store where they bought it. **[T F]**

3. Businesses encourage consumers to return items (**that / what**) they don't like. **[T F]**

2 Conversation

A Listen and Write 45

次の会話を聞いて空所に単語を書きなさい。

M: Hello. I was wondering if it would be possible to return this stereo.
W: Was there something [1](　　　　　) with the stereo?
M: Actually, no. The thing is, I already have a stereo and I don't need this one. I received it as a birthday [2](　　　　　).
W: I see. Do you have the receipt?
M: No. I don't. Is that a [3](　　　　　)?
W: Not really. Although we can't give you a refund for the item [4](　　　　　) a receipt, you can exchange it for another item in the store.

B Listen and Choose 46

質問を聞いて空所に単語を書き、最も適切な答えを (A) ～ (C) から選びなさい。

1. Why does the man (　　　　　) the stereo to the (　　　　　)?
(A) He wants to buy a new one.
(B) He wants the store to fix it.
(C) He wants the store to take back the stereo.

2. Why does the man (　　　　) he (　　　　　)(　　　) return the stereo?
(A) He already has a stereo.
(B) He is not happy with the stereo's sound.
(C) The stereo is broken.

3 Text Completion

次の文章を読んで、空所に入れる最も適切なものを (A) ～ (C) から選びなさい。

Barnes Inc. is dedicated to making you happy. _(1)_ you are not pleased with your purchase, just contact us within 30 days and we will give you a refund. We hope you like our products, but in the event that you _(2)_, we will make returns as painless as possible. Please note that only purchases made directly from us qualify for the 30-day Satisfaction Guarantee. If you purchased your Barnes product from another authorized reseller, _(3)_.

1. (A) Although
   (B) If
   (C) Since

2. (A) aren't
   (B) don't
   (C) haven't

3. (A) please contact that merchant for further details
   (B) please return the product to us for a full refund
   (C) please enjoy your shopping experience with us

4 Composition

A 日本文を参考にして (　　) 内の語句を正しく並べ替えなさい。ただし文頭に来る語も小文字にしてある。

1. In the U.S., it is good for customers (a return policy / guarantees / have / that / that they / to) will be able to easily exchange or return their purchases.
   (アメリカでは購入品を容易に交換したり、返品したりできることを保証する返品ポリシーがあるのは、顧客には良いことです)

   ____

2. (a customer / a number / reasons / of / there are / why) will return a purchase; some are perfectly legitimate, while others may seem a little arbitrary or even dishonest.
   (顧客が買ったものを返品する理由はたくさんありますが、全く妥当なものもあれば、少し恣意的に思えたり不正直とさえ思えるものもあります)

   ____

3. (can be / exchanged / products / purchased / our online shop / via) or returned free of charge within 30 days of customers' receiving them.
   (私たちのオンラインショップで購入した商品は、消費者が受け取って 30 日以内であれば、無料で交換したり返品したりできます)

   ____

B (　　) 内の語句を使って、質問に対する応答文を考えなさい。

1. Have you ever returned an item to a store? What happened?
   (Once, I ordered / online / I realized that)

   ____

2. Second-hand stores and recycle shops are becoming more and more popular in Japan. What do you think about that?
   (great selection / brand name items / reasonably priced)

   ____

Unit 16 Healthcare

日本人の平均寿命は世界でトップクラスですが、その理由の１つに日本の優れた健康保険制度が挙げられます。一方、アメリカでは保険料を払っていない人は、治療を断られることもあり、課題が残されています。

1 Reading 47

Japanese people have one of the longest life-expectancies in the world. One important reason for this is Japan's excellent healthcare system. Japanese hospitals have access to state-of-the-art medical equipment run by proficient medical technicians. Healthcare is reasonable for all Japanese citizens as well as visitors to Japan who have been in the country longer than a year. Hospitals are often owned by physicians and operate as non-profit organizations. Medical costs are covered by the National Health Insurance System, which is paid into by employers and employees. Patients can choose their doctors and cannot be denied treatment. In general, patients pay only part of medical costs, with the remainder covered by the government.

This system is different from the healthcare system in the United States, which is a mix of public and private medical insurance providers. Public healthcare tries to help those most in need – the elderly, the disabled, and the poor. Those who are able to work are expected to apply to one of the many private health insurance companies to cover the workers' medical treatment costs. Unfortunately, the premiums for such coverage can be surprisingly high.

It is estimated that over 30% of Americans are uninsured for healthcare. Because of this, some people even wear identification tags that instruct others NOT to call an ambulance even in the event of an emergency. Disturbingly, those who have no insurance for medical coverage can even be denied treatment.

Currently, the American system is undergoing a series of reforms aimed at making healthcare more affordable. Unfortunately, though, the question in America still remains, "How much are you willing to pay for your health?"

Notes **life-expectancy**「平均寿命」 **healthcare system**「医療制度」 **have access to**「～を利用できる」 **state-of-the-art**「最先端の」 **medical technician**「医療技術者」 **non-profit organization**「非営利団体」 **the National Health Insurance System**「国民健康保険制度」 **medical insurance provider**「医療保険会社」 **identification tag**「認識票」 **medical coverage**「医療保障」

A Vocabulary

次の単語の意味を (a) 〜 (g) から選び、下線上にその記号を書きなさい。

1. proficient ____ (a) a medical doctor
2. physician ____ (b) good at doing something
3. operate ____ (c) not having medical coverage
4. remainder ____ (d) the part that is left over
5. premium ____ (e) the price of insurance
6. uninsured ____ (f) to experience something like a change or test
7. undergo ____ (g) to have control of something; run; manage

B True or False

(　　) 内の適切な単語を選び英文を完成しなさい。次にその英文が本文の内容に合っていればT (True)、間違っていれば F (False) を選びなさい。

1. Healthcare in Japan is comparatively (**affordable / affordability**). **[T F]**

2. In the U.S., if you do not have enough money to pay (**by / for**) medical treatment, a hospital can turn you away. **[T F]**

3. The author believes that a series of (**reform / reforms**) being made to the American healthcare system will make America's system better than Japan's. **[T F]**

2 Conversation

A Listen and Write 48

次の会話を聞いて空所に単語を書きなさい。

W: Thank you for calling Blue Line Health Services. How may I help you?
M: Yes. I'd like to make an appointment to [1] (　　　　　) a doctor.
W: Is there a particular doctor you would like to [2] (　　　　　) with?
M: No. This is my first [3] (　　　　　).
W: I see. When would you like to [4] (　　　　　) in?
M: Well, it's 10 a.m. now; so, anytime in the afternoon.

B Listen and Choose 49

質問を聞いて空所に単語を書き、最も適切な答えを (A) 〜 (C) から選びなさい。

1. (　　　　)(　　　　) the man (　　　　　　　　)?
(A) He wants to buy insurance.
(B) He needs an ambulance.
(C) He wants to make an appointment.

2. (　　　　　)(　　　　　) the man most likely (　　　　　　　) the doctor?
(A) At 10 a.m. (B) At 11 a.m. (C) At 1 p.m.

3 Text Completion

次の文章を読んで、空所に入れる最も適切な語や文を (A) ～ (C) から選びなさい。

Though almost everyone can agree that it is important to maintain your health, one of the things many people tend to overlook is hydration. Our bodies are _(1)_ of 60% water, so it is vital that we make sure we drink enough water every day. Even a 2% decrease in water intake significantly affects how _(2)_ our bodies function. It is recommended that people drink about 3 liters of water daily. _(3)_

1. (A) compose
   (B) composed
   (C) composing
2. (A) best
   (B) good
   (C) well
3. (A) Drinking water is very refreshing.
   (B) This is especially true during the hot and humid summer months.
   (C) Sports drinks are far better than water.

4 Composition

A 日本文を参考にして (　　) 内の語句を正しく並べ替えなさい。

1. Most U.S. citizens have medical insurance, (by / generally / is / provided / the employer / which) and which extends to their family.
   (ほとんどのアメリカ市民は、通常は雇用者によって与えられ、家族に及ぶ健康保険を持っています)

   ____

2. With health insurance, you will be (by / care / entitled / provided / the high-quality / to) the U.S. healthcare system.
   (健康保険があれば、アメリカの医療制度で与えられる質の高い医療を受ける権利があるでしょう)

   ____

3. So far in the U.S., there has been a lack of political (a large role / for / in / support / taking on / the government) controlling healthcare costs.
   (これまでアメリカには、医療費を統制するという大きな役割を政府が果たすための政治的支援がありません)

   ____

B (　　) 内の語句を使って、質問に対する応答文を考えなさい。

1. What do you do to stay healthy?
   (it is important for / do exercise / get enough sleep / stay healthy)

   ____

2. Many people are concerned that the Japanese diet is becoming less healthy? Do you agree or disagree? Why?
   (are eating fast foods / less healthy)

   ____

Unit 17 Vending Machines

外国の人が日本で驚くのは、自販機の圧倒的な台数、そして自販機が扱う商品の種類の多さです。狭い場所で多くの収益を上げていますが、自販機が日本で流行る理由を考えてみましょう。

1 Reading 50

Want a can of hot coffee? How about a bagel for breakfast? Have you forgotten your partner's birthday? What about a bouquet of flowers? Feel like watching a DVD? No problem. There's always a vending machine available to save the day! Foreigners in Japan are often surprised by what is available in vending machines, as vending machines overseas provide little more than beverages and snacks. They are also shocked by how prevalent these machines are. There are over 5 million vending machines in Japan (about one machine for every 23 people), selling a vast assortment of merchandise.

For various reasons, Japan is the perfect country for vending machines. As Japan continues to struggle with a dwindling workforce, vending machines provide services without requiring someone to serve you. In addition, whereas places like America and Canada have a population that is spread over a wide area, Japan has one of the world's highest population densities. Because of this, real estate is at a premium. By providing service to so many people living in such a crowded place, vending machines can generate more revenue from each square meter of land than traditional retail stores. In fact, vending machines generate over ¥7 trillion in sales annually.

Once primarily cash-based, vending machines have adapted in response to advancing technology and the emerging movement toward non-cash payments. Many vending machines now accept various forms of electronic payment.

Perhaps one of the most important reasons that vending machines are so popular in Japan is public safety. Japan boasts one of the world's lowest rates of vandalism and property crime. In places like America, most companies would never even consider placing a stand-alone vending machine in a public place because of the danger of theft and damage.

Notes **save the day**「急場を救う」 **a vast assortment of**「～の多くの品揃え」 **dwindling workforce**「減少する労働力」 **population density**「人口密度」 **retail store**「小売店」 **cash-based**「現金主義の」 **in response to**「～に対応して」 **emerging movement**「新たな動き」 **electronic payment**「電子決済」 **property crime**「窃盗犯罪」 **stand-alone**「孤立する」

A Vocabulary

次の単語の意味を (a) ～ (g) から選び、下線上にその記号を書きなさい。

1. bagel _____ (a) a bread roll shaped like a ring
2. struggle _____ (b) a price that is higher than the regular price
3. premium _____ (c) money made by a business or government
4. revenue _____ (d) the act of destroying public property
5. generate _____ (e) to have a difficult time
6. boast _____ (f) to talk too proudly; brag
7. vandalism _____ (g) to produce something

B True or False

(　　) 内の適切な語句を選び英文を完成しなさい。次にその英文が本文の内容に合っていれば T (True)、間違っていれば F (False) を選びなさい。

1. Visitors to Japan are often surprised (**at / to**) how hard it is to find vending machines. **[T F]**

2. In Japan, companies often use vending machines because the machines are so cost-(**effective / effectively**). **[T F]**

3. Vending machines are less popular in the U.S. (**because / because of**) most sellers are concerned about crime, especially vandalism. **[T F]**

2 Conversation

A Listen and Write 51

次の会話を聞いて空所に単語を書きなさい。

M: Honey. Do you know if this jar is burnable or non-burnable?
W: That one is burnable.
M: How [1](　　　　　) this one? Is this burnable, too?
W: No. That one is non-burnable.
M: How can you tell the [2](　　　　　　　)? They're both jars.
W: Well, that jar was [3](　　　　　) for jam and the other is my old make-up jar. I guess the [4](　　　　　　　) way to tell the difference is to see whether or not a jar was used for food.

B Listen and Choose 52

質問を聞いて空所に単語を書き、最も適切な答えを (A) ～ (C) から選びなさい。

1. What is the man (　　　　　　　)(　　　　　)?
(A) How to separate the garbage.
(B) Where to throw the garbage away.
(C) What to put in the jars.

2. How does the woman (　　　　　) what is burnable (　　　　) what is not burnable?
(A) Whether or not the jar is big or small.
(B) Whether or not the jar is plastic or glass.
(C) Whether or not the jar was used for food.

3 Text Completion

次の文章を読んで、空所に入れる最も適切なものを (A) ～ (C) から選びなさい。

Visitors to Japan quickly become annoyed when they try to find trash cans in public. It can be frustrating for them to have to carry around used wrappers _(1)_ they can find a suitable place to dispose of their trash. Although strict garbage laws are one reason for the low number of public trash cans in Japan, perhaps the main reason is public _(2)_. Many public trash cans have been pulled off the streets because they are seen as being potential hiding places for hazardous chemicals. Yet, despite the lack of public trash cans, _(3)_.

1. (A) as if
   (B) until
   (C) when

2. (A) safe
   (B) safely
   (C) safety

3. (A) Japan is still a safe country
   (B) Japan's streets remain cluttered with trash
   (C) Japan's streets remain relatively litter-free

4 Composition

A 日本文を参考にして (　　) 内の語句を正しく並べ替えなさい。ただし文頭に来る語も小文字にしてある。

1. (every tourist / is / notices / one thing / that / to Japan) the large number of vending machines at stations and inside buildings.
   (日本に来るすべての旅行者が気付くことの１つは、駅や建物内にあるたくさんの自販機です)

2. Foreigners will stumble (a vending machine / matter / no / upon / they're / where) going or happen to be.
   (外国人はたとえどこに行っても、たまたまどこにいても、自販機に出くわすでしょう)

3. Vending machines are considered convenient because customers are able (need / they / them / things / to buy / whenever).
   (自販機は、顧客が必要なときはいつでも品物を買うことができるので、便利だと考えられます)

B (　　) 内の語句を使って、質問に対する応答文を考えなさい。

1. What it is the strangest item you have seen sold in a vending machine?
   (The oddest thing / a cup of noodles / I wondered if)

2. Some people say that as Japan becomes more globalized, it will become a target for global problems such as terrorism. What do you think about that?
   (The more Japan becomes..., the more / target for acts of terror / cyber theft)

Unit 18 Toilets

世界のトイレ文化をリードする日本のウォシュレットトイレには、外国の人が「アッ」と驚く最先端の科学技術が投入されています。世界のトイレ事情について考えてみましょう。

1 Reading 53

Japanese toilets are remarkable pieces of technology. However, for foreigners visiting Japan, these toilets, which are often called "washlets," can be intimidating, what with all their panels of buttons, strange symbols, and ambiguous stickmen drawings explaining how to use them. It is estimated that 81% of Japanese households now have washlets, which have also become increasingly common in many public restrooms. This kind of convenience is by no means commonplace in other countries.

Though many places in China have been installing more "Western style" toilets, many places still have old-style squat toilets similar to those once found all over Japan. It is not uncommon to find that squat toilets in China are really little more than a hole in the floor – and that they usually have no door for privacy. Moreover, many of these toilets are unisex, used by both males and females.

When you visit countries like Cuba and the Philippines, don't be surprised to find that public restrooms often have no toilet paper. Other countries like Mexico have toilet paper, but because of the poor plumbing, flushing paper down the toilet can clog or even break the pipes. To address this, Mexico's public washrooms have a small trash bin where you can dispose of your toilet paper when you are done.

Not every country so generously provides free public restrooms. In Sweden, people commonly must pay to use a public restroom. The money is used to keep the facilities clean. In Spain and Italy, finding a public toilet is a challenge. People will often use the facilities provided in bars, cafes, restaurants, or shops. If you do find a restroom, you might be surprised to see two different kinds of bowls. One is meant for doing your business, while the other is used to clean yourself up after. Make sure you choose wisely.

Notes **stickman drawing**「棒人間の絵」 **public restroom**「公衆トイレ」 **by no means**「決して～でない」 **western style**「洋式の」 **squat toilet**「和式トイレ」 **not uncommon**「珍しくない」 **little more than**「～にすぎない」 **trash bin**「ゴミ箱」 **do one's business**「用を足す」

A Vocabulary

次の単語の意味を (a) ～ (g) から選び、下線上にその記号を書きなさい。

1. intimidating ____ (a) appearing in many places, not unusual
2. ambiguous ____ (b) equipment or place that is built for a specific purpose
3. commonplace ____ (c) making you feel nervous or frightened
4. address ____ (d) not expressed or understood clearly; vague
5. flush ____ (e) to become blocked or stuck
6. clog ____ (f) to clean something with a flow of water
7. facility ____ (g) to deal with a problem

B True or False

(　　) 内の適切な単語を選び英文を完成しなさい。次にその英文が本文の内容に合っていれば T (True)、間違っていれば F (False) を選びなさい。

1. Most visitors to Japan find Japan's modern new toilets (**easy / easily**) to use. **[T F]**
2. Visitors to China will (**rare / rarely**) find toilets that look like holes in the floor. **[T F]**
3. In Spain, public restrooms can often be (**difficult / difficulty**) to find. **[T F]**

2 Conversation

A Listen and Write 54

次の会話を聞いて空所に単語を書きなさい。

W: You look pale. Are you okay?
M: Can I [1](　　　　) your restroom?
W: Sure. It's down the [2](　　　　) on your left. Across from the study. Are you sure you're okay?
M: Yeah. I think it's something I [3](　　　　).
W: I hope it isn't something I made.
M: No. I was hungry and [4](　　　　) for some fast food on the way here.

B Listen and Choose 55

質問を聞いて空所に単語を書き、最も適切な答えを (A) ～ (C) から選びなさい。

1. What is probably (　　　　)(　　　　) the man?
(A) He has a headache.
(B) He has a stomachache.
(C) He's hungry.

2. Why does the man think he is (　　　　)(　　　　)?
(A) Because he ate some fast food.
(B) Because he ate the woman's cooking.
(C) Because he hasn't eaten for a long time.

3 Text Completion

次の文章を読んで、空所に入れる最も適切な語句や文を (A) ～ (C) から選びなさい。

Toilet paper had its origins in China in the 14th century. The first commercial toilet paper, _(1)_ to what we use today, wasn't invented until the mid-19th century. So, what did people use before toilet paper? Depending on the country, climate, and the resources available, various materials _(2)_ to take care of people's toilet needs. Some things people used were leaves, grass, fruit peels, moss, and even sea shells! Those with money would often use wool or hemp. Some of these old toilet practices are still in use today. _(3)_

1. (A) similar
   (B) similarly
   (C) similarity

2. (A) used
   (B) were used
   (C) were using

3. (A) In Ancient Rome, Romans would use sponges scented with rose water.
   (B) In India, for example, the practice of washing up after yourself using your left hand is still quite commonly practiced.
   (C) It was the French invented the bidet in the 17th century.

4 Composition

A 日本文を参考にして (　　) 内の語句を正しく並べ替えなさい。

1. When you travel abroad, you will often (a problem / cultural / differences / face / of / regarding) restroom use.
   (海外旅行をするとき、トイレの使用に関する文化の違いの問題によく直面するでしょう)

2. Public toilets in Japan are free and (almost / are located / easy / since / to find, / they) everywhere.
   (日本では公衆トイレは無料で、ほとんどどこにでもあるので見つけるのが容易です)

3. Toilets in Japan are kept (comfort / ensure / for / spotlessly clean / the utmost / to) anyone who uses them.
   (日本のトイレは、使用する誰に対しても最高の快適さを保証するために、汚れひとつないぐらい、きれいにされています)

B (　　) 内の語句を使って、質問に対する応答文を考えなさい。

1. In Taiwan, there is a popular restaurant called *Modern Toilet* that serves food in dishes that look like toilet bowls. Would you like to eat there?
   (gross experience / scooping out / from a toilet bowl)

2. Some people believe that Japanese washlets are becoming too fancy. What do you think about that?
   (newer-model washlets / a bit of an extravagance / all those functions)

Unit 19 Rapid Transit Systems

日本を象徴するものの１つが新幹線です。信頼、安全、快適さで世界中の国々から羨望の眼差しで見られています。しかし、なぜアメリカでは高速鉄道が発展しないのでしょうか。

1 Reading 56

One of the most iconic images of modern Japan is a bullet train speeding past Mount Fuji. Japan's high-speed rapid transit system celebrated its 50th anniversary in 2014. Over that half century, the system saw many dramatic advancements. The 500-kilometer service between Tokyo and Shin-Osaka, which originally took 3 hours and 10 minutes, can now be traveled in just over 2 hours! Amazingly, Japan's high-speed rapid transit system has never had a passenger fatality or injury due to an accident. Is it any wonder that this transportation system is the envy of many countries around the world for its speed, reliability, comfort, and safety?

So, why is there no high-speed rapid-transit system in the U.S.? It's not that there is no need. Many people spend hours each day commuting between their home and work. One reason for this lack is that the U.S. has developed in a different way than Japan. America has a strong and well-developed automobile culture. Americans love their cars, and the government injects billions of dollars into maintaining the highway system. Another reason is the suburban sprawl that marks the American landscape. In addition, there is also the importance of property rights.

Unlike the concentrated residential and mixed zoning areas of Japan and Europe, in the U.S. houses are spread out in residential clusters that are far from central transportation hubs. This makes it difficult to find suitable locations to build transit stations. Even when there is a station, people still need a vehicle to get to and from it.

Having lived in Japan for several years, I have come to appreciate just how convenient Japan's rail system is. How glad I am that I can go from point to point much faster and with less hassle than I would be able to if I were driving a car!

Notes **rapid transit system**「高速輸送システム」 **iconic image**「象徴的イメージ」 **bullet train**「新幹線」 **well-developed**「よく発達した」 **suburban sprawl**「都市のスプロール現象」郊外へ拡大すること **property right**「財産権」 **zoning area**「都市計画地域」 **go from point to point**「あちこちに行く」

A Vocabulary

次の単語の意味を (a) ～ (g) から選び、下線上にその記号を書きなさい。

1. concentrated ____ (a) a death that results from an accident
2. advancement ____ (b) densely populated; crowded
3. fatality ____ (c) progress to a higher stage; development
4. commute ____ (d) something that causes trouble
5. landscape ____ (e) the visible features of an area
6. inject ____ (f) to provide something needed
7. hassle ____ (g) to travel regularly to and from work or school

B True or False

(　　) 内の適切な語句を選び英文を完成しなさい。次にその英文が本文の内容に合っていれば T (True)、間違っていれば F (False) を選びなさい。

1. There has never been a death (**for / from**) an accident on the bullet train. **[T F]**
2. One reason there is no high-speed transit system in the U.S. is that people tend (**living / to live**) far from city centers. **[T F]**
3. According to the author, Japan's transit system is fast but (**inconvenient / inconvenience**). **[T F]**

2 Conversation

A Listen and Write 57

次の会話を聞いて空所に単語を書きなさい。

M: What are you doing for the long weekend?
W: I'm planning on [1](　　　　　) up to Hokkaido to visit some friends.
M: Flying? Why not take the bullet train? It goes all the [2](　　　　　) up to Hakodate now.
W: Yeah, but it's more [3](　　　　　　　), and it takes such a long time.
M: But I heard the cars are beautiful and so comfortable, and to be honest, I am a big fan of the lunch [4](　　　　　) they serve on the trains.
W: Yeah, I suppose so. Okay. Thanks for the suggestion. I'll sleep on it.

B Listen and Choose 58

質問を聞いて空所に単語を書き、最も適切な答えを (A) ～ (C) から選びなさい。

1. (　　　　　) is the woman (　　　　　　　)(　　　　　) do for the long weekend?
(A) She wants to go sightseeing in Hokkaido.
(B) She wants to ride the new bullet train to Hokkaido.
(C) She wants to visit some friends in Hokkaido.

2. Why does the man (　　　　　　　)(　　　　　　　) the bullet train?
(A) The bullet train is cheaper and faster.
(B) The bullet train is comfortable and has delicious food.
(C) The bullet train is not so crowded.

3 Text Completion

次の図表を見て、空所に入れる最も適切な語句を (A) ～ (C) から選びなさい。

	TRANSPORTATION		POPULATION	
Country	Total High-speed Transit System (kms)	Car Owners (% of population)	Total Population (million)	Population Living in Urban Area (%)
Austria	502	59	8.4	68
China	37,156	13	1,357.0	56
France	2,793	58	65.8	86
Germany	1,762	59	80.6	74
Italy	1,048	68	60.7	68
Japan	3,446	59	127.3	91
Russia	1,415	32	143.5	74
the U.K.	1,377	52	64.6	84
the U.S.	28	81	321.1	82

1. According to the table above, _(1)_ has the lowest percentage of car owners.
   (A) China (B) Russia (C) the U.K.
2. According to the table above, _(2)_ has the most people living in or near a major city.
   (A) Austria (B) France (C) Japan
3. If it is true that the percentage of car owners is inversely related to high-speed rail systems, you would expect to find the shortest high-speed rail system in _(3)_.
   (A) Germany (B) Italy (C) the U.S.

4 Composition

A 日本文を参考にして (　　) 内の語句を正しく並べ替えなさい。

1. The bullet train, (being / high-speed / in / rapid / the first / train) the world, is Japan's pride and joy.
   (世界で最初の高速鉄道である新幹線は、日本の誇りと喜びです)

2. The bullet train achieves its high speeds through (an aerodynamic / and technology / designed / of / shape / the use) to maximize power.
   (新幹線は、パワーを最大限にするために設計された流線型と技術の使用で、最高スピードを達成しています)

3. The world-renowned bullet train offers the world's safest and (comfort / match / most reliable / the train's peerless / to / transport system).
   (世界的に有名な新幹線は、列車のこの上ない快適さに合う、世界で最も安全で最も信頼できる輸送システムを提供しています)

B (　　) 内の語句を使って、質問に対する応答文を考えなさい。

1. Traveling around Japan, would you rather fly or take the bullet train? Why?
   (is preferable to / excellent way / beautiful Japanese scenery)

2. To improve security, Japan Railways is thinking about using armed security guards on their trains. What do you think about that?
   (make trains safe / On the other hand, / anxious and uncomfortable)

Unit 20 Cables in the Sky

外国の人が日本でビックリするものの１つは、地上のいたるところで、ごちゃごちゃクモの巣のように張り巡らされている電線です。西洋では通例、電線を地中に埋めます。そのメリットとデメリットを考えてみましょう。

1 Reading 59

While on a tour of Japan, a friend of mine commented, “Wow! Japan is so messy.” Surprised, I asked what she meant, and she replied, “Look at all the cables. They’re everywhere!”

Having lived in Japan for so long, I had gotten used to what she was referring to. Looking up at the sky, I couldn’t help but notice the web of cables crisscrossing streets and hanging between buildings. This is of course particularly true of large cosmopolitan cities like Tokyo and Osaka. Unlike many countries in Europe and North America, Japan has predominantly aboveground power lines. In Canada, for example, the majority of power and communication cables have been placed underground. Because of extreme weather, underground cables are preferred for their reliability and protection from the elements. Many new urban developments use underground cables because they create less visual clutter and require only a narrow strip of land to install.

Though Japan is also prone to extreme environmental conditions, particularly typhoons and earthquakes, much of Japan’s power grid remains aboveground. Only 7% of Tokyo, for example, has subterranean cables, with Osaka having much less. One reason is that it is difficult to do construction work in developments that exist in cramped spaces. Other reasons are that it is easier to identify problems in an aboveground power system, and that the poles used can be multipurposed to provide locations for putting up street lights and signage. Some residents even prefer the “rustic” look of the poles and cables.

Many people, myself included, would like to see the visual clutter reduced. However, with so many different things requiring power, like small ramen shops and vending machines on every corner – aboveground poles and cables will probably remain a distinct part of the Japanese landscape.

Notes **can’t help but**「～せざるを得ない」 **aboveground power line**「地上送電線」 **communication cable**「通信ケーブル」 **extreme weather**「異常気象」 **urban development**「都市開発」 **a narrow strip of land**「細長い土地」 **power grid**「送電網」 **subterranean cable**「地下ケーブル」 **multipurposed**「多目的の」

A Vocabulary

次の単語の意味を (a) ～ (g) から選び、下線上にその記号を書きなさい。

1. messy ____ (a) describing the simple style of the countryside
2. cosmopolitan ____ (b) mainly; primarily
3. elements ____ (c) not clean or tidy
4. construct ____ (d) of a city populated by people around the world
5. identify ____ (e) weather; especially bad weather
6. predominantly ____ (f) to find out what is wrong; determine; name
7. rustic ____ (g) to build or make something

B True or False

(　　) 内の適切な語句を選び英文を完成しなさい。次にその英文が本文の内容に合っていれば T (True)、間違っていれば F (False) を選びなさい。

1. The author's friend felt that Japan was messy because there (**was / were**) so much garbage cluttering the streets. **[T F]**

2. In Canada, power cables are usually installed below ground because underground cables are cleaner looking and more (**resistance / resistant**) to the elements. **[T F]**

3. The author feels that more should be done in Japan (**removing / to remove**) aboveground power lines. **[T F]**

2 Conversation

A Listen and Write 60

次の会話を聞いて空所に単語を書きなさい。

M: Did you hear? There is a typhoon warning for the area this afternoon.
W: Really? I'd better [1](　　　　　) with the school to see if classes have been cancelled.
M: Okay. While you do that, I'll take the kids to the grocery store and pick up some [2](　　　　　).
W: Good idea. Don't forget to buy some water. I [3](　　　　　) the batteries in the flashlight last week, but I think we'll need some for the radio.
M: Right. Anything else?
W: Oh, yes! Maybe you should [4](　　　　　) up some snacks and lunch boxes in case the power goes out again.

B Listen and Choose 61

質問を聞いて空所に単語を書き、最も適切な答えを (A) ～ (C) から選びなさい。

1. Why will the woman (　　　　　) the (　　　　　)?
(A) To ask the school if her children are safe.
(B) To check if classes are cancelled.
(C) To tell the school that a typhoon is coming.

2. Why does the woman (　　　　　) the man (　　　)(　　　　　) snacks and lunch boxes?
(A) She doesn't think she will have time to cook.
(B) She is concerned that her children might get hungry.
(C) She is worried that there might be a loss of power.

3 Text Completion

次の文章を読んで、空所に入れる最も適切な語句や文を (A) ～ (C) から選びなさい。

Visual pollution is a problem that faces many large cities around the world. It occurs _(1)_ large billboards, overhead power lines, cellphone towers, and other similar features mar a city's landscape. A plethora of signage and unsightly advertising has a negative impact not only on the environment _(2)_ on citizens' safety and mental health. The visual environment is as essential to a city as clean water and air. Because of this, many large cities have begun cracking down on visual pollution. _(3)_

1. (A) how
   (B) when
   (C) why

2. (A) as well as
   (B) but also
   (C) in case

3. (A) They are paying businesses to replace signs that have been broken or destroyed with larger, more attractive ones.
   (B) They are too short of funding to do anything at all about this problem.
   (C) They have passed laws that restrict the size and placement of outdoor advertising.

4 Composition

A 日本文を参考にして (　　) 内の語句を正しく並べ替えなさい。

1. Utility poles and overhead power lines (a common / are / feature / in / of / the landscape) most parts of Japan, and often can ruin a lovely vista.
   (電柱と頭上の送電線は、日本のほとんどの場所の風景のありふれた特徴で、きれいな風景をしばしば台無しにします)

   ____

2. The aboveground power grid is cheaper to repair, and when disaster strikes, aboveground lines are (bring back / condition / easier / good / into / to).
   (地上の送電網は修理するのが安く、災害が起こったとき、地上の電線は復旧するのが容易です)

   ____

3. In general, the installation of underground power lines of the same voltage and distance costs up (of / overhead lines / several / that / times / to).
   (一般に地中送電線の設置は、同じ電圧と距離で地上架線の数倍もの費用がかかります)

   ____

B (　　) 内の語句を使って、質問に対する応答文を考えなさい。

1. Do you agree with the author's friend that "Japan is so messy"? Why or why not?
   (a plastic bag / had spilled on the street / bottles of milk)

   ____

2. To meet the electricity demands of the population, Japan uses nuclear energy. What do you think about that?
   (benefits and disadvantages / supply enough energy / too dangerous)

   ____

Unit 21 Tissue Marketing

日本の駅前や街中を歩くと、広告の入ったポケットティッシュが配られています。外国の人にはティシュ配りは驚きの日本文化でしたが、今、日本発祥のティッシュ文化は世界に徐々に浸透しています。

1 Reading 62

Walking through any major city in Japan, you will inevitably see people handing out free pocket tissues with advertising inside. This kind of “guerilla marketing” started in Japan in the 1960s and has become increasingly common. Now, over four billion tissues are distributed annually, generating an estimated ¥75 billion or more in sales. Costing only 10 to 25 yen to produce and hand out, this unique-to-Japan method is a cost-effective way for businesses to connect with potential customers. Studies show that over 75% of people who accept tissues read the advertisements inside. Why? Some hope that they will find nice discounts, while others feel it is rude not to look.

Traditionally, North American businesses tend to frown upon such “loss leaders,” that is, providing items below cost to attract consumers and encourage them to buy other products. Giving things away for “free” is even less acceptable. Instead, companies generally have preferred to reward patronage by offering amenities and add-on products only after customers have purchased an item. Despite this, the success of Japan’s guerilla marketing strategy has caused many overseas businesses, especially startups, to reconsider.

In 2000, the practice was introduced to Canada after a Canadian businessman saw tissue advertising while on a business trip to Japan. In 2005, one of Japan’s largest trading companies introduced the practice in New York. Promoting a Broadway musical, 10,000 tissue packs were distributed to people on the street, generating $150,000 in ticket sales. Since this initial success, the practice has spread to other parts of the country.

In 2007, the first advertising campaign using tissues was launched in the U.K. to promote a nonprofit organization. Whether or not tissue marketing will be as successful overseas as it has been in Japan is still up for debate. However, one thing is certain: Tissue marketing in Japan will not disappear anytime soon.

Notes **hand out**「配る」 **guerilla marketing**「ゲリラマーケティング」低コストでの広告戦略 **cost-effective way**「費用効率の良いやり方」 **loss leader**「ロスリーダー」特売品 **even less**「まして〜でない」 **amenity**「アメニティグッズ」 **add-on product**「追加商品」 **startup**「ベンチャー企業」 **initial success**「最初の成功」 **nonprofit organization**「非営利団体」 **be still up for debate**「まだ議論の余地がある」

A Vocabulary

次の単語の意味を (a) ～ (g) から選び、下線上にその記号を書きなさい。

1. inevitably ____ (a) a method or plan for achieving a goal
2. potential ____ (b) a pleasant or useful product
3. patronage ____ (c) capable of becoming real; possible
4. amenity ____ (d) certain to happen; unavoidably
5. strategy ____ (e) customer support given to a business
6. launch ____ (f) to start or initiate
7. disappear ____ (g) to stop existing; pass out of sight

B True or False

(　　) 内の適切な単語を選び英文を完成しなさい。次にその英文が本文の内容に合っていれば T (True)、間違っていれば F (False) を選びなさい。

1. "Guerrilla marketing" refers to a marketing strategy (**that / what**) was invented in Japan. **[T F]**

2. North American businesses typically give products away for (**free / freely**). **[T F]**

3. The author feels that tissue marketing will continue to be (**popular / popularity**) in Japan. **[T F]**

2 Conversation

A Listen and Write 63

次の会話を聞いて、空所に単語を書きなさい。

M: ACHOO!
W: Bless you! Are you OK?
M: Yes. Thank you. Sorry about [1](　　　　　).
W: Do you have a [2](　　　　　)?
M: No, I don't think so. I think it's hay [3](　　　　　). I usually get it around this time every year. This year, though, it's really bad. ACHOO!
W: Wow. Here. Take this tissue. You'll probably [4](　　　　　) it later.

B Listen and Choose 64

質問を聞いて空所に単語を書き、最も適切な答えを (A) ～ (C) から選びなさい。

1. (　　　　)(　　　　　) the woman (　　　　) "Bless you"?
(A) Because the man felt chilly.
(B) Because the man got well.
(C) Because the man sneezed.

2. (　　　　　　　)(　　　) the man, (　　　　　) does he get every year?
(A) Allergies. (B) A cold. (C) A high temperature.

3 Text Completion

次の文章を読んで、空所に入れる最も適切な語や文を (A) ～ (C) から選びなさい。

Most people have heard or even used the saying "Bless you" when someone sneezes. Where does this expression come from? There are many stories _(1)_ its origin. One of the most interesting stems from the superstition that when someone sneezes, their soul_(2)_ leaves their body. This creates an opportunity for evil spirits to come rushing in. So, people would say "Bless you" as a way to ward off evil spirits. _(3)_ We continue to say "Bless you" out of habit.

1. (A) concerning
   (B) related
   (C) with regard

2. (A) temporal
   (B) temporary
   (C) temporarily

3. (A) In the past, people foolishly believed evil spirits were everywhere.
   (B) Nowadays, however, we know much more about why we sneeze.
   (C) People often sneeze because they have a cold or an allergy.

4 Composition

A 日本文を参考にして (　　) 内の語句を正しく並べ替えなさい。

1. The cost of producing a packet of tissue is low, (companies / for / makes / suitable / the marketing concept / which) with limited budgets.
   (袋入りティッシュを作る価格は安く、そのことがマーケティングコンセプトを予算が限られた会社に相応しいものにしています)

2. Unlike advertisement flyers, which are almost always immediately thrown away, pocket tissue advertisements are (all the tissues / are / usually kept / until / up / used).
   (ほとんどいつもすぐに捨てられる広告チラシとは異なり、ポケットティッシュ広告はたいてい、すべてのティッシュを使い切るまで保持されています)

3. Businesses can (a big / big / grab / market share / spending / without) dollars to put the tissue advertising strategy into practice.
   (会社は、ティッシュ広告戦略を実行するのに大金を使わないで、大きなマーケットシェアをつかむことができます)

B (　　) 内の語句を使って、質問に対する応答文を考えなさい。

1. Have you ever received a free packet of tissues? If so, did you read or use the advertisement inside?
   (once in a blue moon / throw the ad / trash bin)

2. Many people complain that advertisements and commercials depict an unrealistic view of life. Alcohol ads, for example, portray drinking as elegant. Do you agree or disagree? Why?
   (a little unrealistic / healthy and happy / drink alcohol / go away)

Unit 22 PDA

一般に、日本人は感情を抑えます。特に愛情表現を街頭などの人前ですることは、はばかられます。公共の場での愛情表現については、寛大な国もあれば、厳しい規制のある国もあり、様々です。

1 Reading 65

Foreigners who visit Japan often comment that Japanese are “emotionally repressed.” One reason for this is the Japanese attitude to public displays of affection, or PDA. Though PDA is not forbidden in Japan, most Japanese would balk at doing things like kissing, hugging, or holding hands on the street. Understandably, since Japanese culture places much emphasis on emotional reserve, expressing feelings, particularly in a public setting, will most likely shock Japanese bystanders and bring about a few disapproving glances. In fact, the Japanese attitude toward PDA is by no means extreme: Many other countries have a much more severe reaction to PDA.

India, for example, bans all PDA. According to India’s Penal Code, PDA is a crime, and those engaging in a little outdoor smooching can, if caught, face large fines or even spend time in prison. At the other end of the spectrum are countries like Italy, France, and Spain, where it is not uncommon to witness a couple tangled up in an intimate embrace in public in broad daylight. Interestingly, though many Canadians – who are by nature a very touchy-feely people – may see Japan as too restrictive, they may also think that European affection is a little too permissive.

In Japan, a country where sex shops and love hotels can be found almost everywhere, it strikes many foreigners as a little strange that something as simple as giving your partner a peck on the cheek can be viewed with such disdain. However, if you are a foreigner living in Japan, it’s important for you to understand and respect the culture you are living in – and to keep your public make-out sessions to a minimum. Better yet, save them until you get behind closed doors.

Notes **PDA**「公共の場での愛情表現」 **balk at**「～をためらう」 **in a public setting**「公共の場で」 **Penal Code**「刑法」 **tangle up**「抱き合う」 **in broad daylight**「真昼間に」 **by nature**「生来」 **touchy-feely**「いちゃつく」 **sex shop**「風俗店」 **give one’s partner a peck on the cheek**「恋人の頬に軽くキスをする」 **make-out sessions**「いちゃつく時間」

A Vocabulary

次の単語の意味を (a) ～ (g) から選び、下線上にその記号を書きなさい。

1. repress _____ (a) a feeling of strong dislike
2. bystander _____ (b) a person present at an event but who doesn't take part
3. embrace _____ (c) being too limiting or controlling
4. restrictive _____ (d) fondness or love
5. affection _____ (e) giving people a lot of freedom of behavior
6. permissive _____ (f) the act of holding someone in your arms; hug
7. disdain _____ (g) to stop, control, or not show your feelings

B True or False

(　　) 内の適切な単語を選び英文を完成しなさい。次にその英文が本文の内容に合っていれば T (True)、間違っていれば F (False) を選びなさい。

1. Japanese seem to find (**it / they**) difficult to express their emotions. **[T F]**
2. In India, kissing in public is (**considered / considering**) a crime. **[T F]**
3. The author seems to agree (**about / with**) the old adage, "When in Rome, do as the Romans do," which means to respect the places you visit. **[T F]**

2 Conversation

A Listen and Write 66

次の会話を聞いて空所に単語を書きなさい。

M: Hey, Marissa! Were you downtown yesterday?
W: Yes. Why?
M: I thought I saw you 1(　　　　　) along 5th Avenue with a guy. Is he your new boyfriend?
W: Why would you say that?
M: Well, you seemed pretty close, and you were holding 2(　　　　　)!
W: You saw that? I am so 3(　　　　　)!
M: Don't be. You two made a very 4(　　　　　) couple. So, what's he like?

B Listen and Choose 67

質問を聞いて空所に単語を書き、最も適切な答えを (A) ～ (C) から選びなさい。

1. Why did the man (　　　　) the woman (　　　　)(　　　　) had been yesterday?
(A) He thought he might have seen her.
(B) He had wanted to ask her for some help.
(C) He had trouble contacting her.

2. Why does the man (　　　　) the woman (　　　　)(　　　　) new boyfriend?
(A) Because she and the guy seemed very friendly with each other.
(B) Because the guy was so attractive.
(C) Because he had seen the guy before.

3 Text Completion

次の文章を読んで、空所に入れる最も適切な語や文を (A) ～ (C) から選びなさい。

Two strangers see each other across a crowded room. Their eyes meet, and both feel an electricity going back and forth _(1)_ them. As melodramatic as this may sound, many people really do believe in love at first sight. Now, researchers in the Netherlands have found that there just may be _(2)_ evidence to support the idea. The researchers discovered some interesting things. Love at first sight is usually not mutual. _(3)_ People say that they experienced love at first sight more with people they find physically attractive than with those whom they find interesting.

1. (A) among
   (B) between
   (C) within

2. (A) science
   (B) scientific
   (C) scientist

3. (A) Both men and women generally don't believe in the idea.
   (B) Men experience love at first sight as much as women do.
   (C) Men feel love at first sight more often than women do.

4 Composition

A 日本文を参考にして (　　) 内の語句を正しく並べ替えなさい。ただし文頭に来る語も小文字にしてある。

1. (affection / an acceptable / display / is / of / what) varies from culture to culture.
   (何が受け入れられる愛情表現かということは、文化によって異なります)

   ____

2. In Japan, (declare / if / love / to someone / you / your), they might not respond to you immediately.
   (日本では誰かに愛を告白しても、あなたにすぐに返事をしないかもしれません)

   ____

3. Most Japanese give you a strange look if (in / much affection / show / to / you / your partner) public.
   (ほとんどの日本人は、人前でパートナーに多くの愛情を示すと、けげんな目であなたを見ます)

   ____

B (　　) 内の語句を使って、質問に対する応答文を考えなさい。

1. Do you believe in love at first sight? Why?
   (might be attracted to / fall in love with / time goes on)

   ____

2. Online dating has become popular among young adults these days. Do you think that online dating will become more or less popular in the future? Why or why not?
   (find a suitable match / incorrect information / profiles)

   ____

Unit 23 Love Hotels

ラブホテルは外国から来た観光客を魅了する日本特有の文化の１つです。海外にはほとんど存在しませんが、アメリカにはそれに似たノーテルモーテルがあります。

1 Reading 68

With their fancy lettering, gigantic signs, and provocative names, love hotels can be found all over Japan. Unlike ordinary hotels, as a way to give guest privacy, love hotels have few windows. They also have concealed parking lots so guests can come and go without being seen. Inside, the rooms are also spacious, far larger than most apartments found in cities like Tokyo and Osaka. In addition to their regular amenities, love hotels often provide various luxurious facilities, including Jacuzzis, large screen TVs, karaoke machines, and even exercise equipment! What really makes love hotels so fascinating are the over-the-top designs and decors that one can find in the rooms.

Love hotels are not unique to Japan. Similar establishments can be found in North America, where they are known as "no-tell motels." These short-stay lodgings are usually located just off a highway and are normally used for the same purposes as Japan's love hotels. The rooms are generally small and have few amenities outside of a shower, TV, and (if you are lucky) a vibrating bed. These no-tell motels are nowhere near as ubiquitous as their Japanese counterparts, nor do they boast the outlandish decors of the rooms found in Japan. In contrast, couples can choose to enjoy themselves against the backdrop of a medieval castle, pirate ship, hospital room – or even a view of outer space in Japan's love hotels.

These days, because love hotels are not as popular as they used to be, many are marketing themselves as regular accommodations. As a matter of fact, the next time I'm looking for a convenient place to stay, I just might take advantage of what these "new" love hotels have to offer and treat myself to a relaxing night on a king-size bed in a room decorated like an undersea kingdom.

Notes **concealed parking lot**「隠された駐車場」 **Jacuzzi**「ジャクジー」気泡がでる泡風呂 **over-the-top design**「過度のデザイン」 **no-tell motel**「ノーテルモーテル」ラブホテルに似たもの **nowhere near**「到底～ない」 **against the backdrop of**「～を背景に」 **outer space**「宇宙」 **take advantage of**「～を利用する」 **treat oneself to**「自分自身に～のご褒美を与える」 **undersea kingdom**「海底王国」

A Vocabulary

次の単語の意味を (a) ～ (g) から選び、下線上にその記号を書きなさい。

1. gigantic ____ (a) a place where a person can stay for a short time
2. provocative ____ (b) causing strong feelings or sexual excitement
3. concealed ____ (c) existing in large numbers; found everywhere
4. accommodation ____ (d) extremely large
5. ubiquitous ____ (e) hidden; out of sight
6. counterpart ____ (f) something that has the same function as another
7. backdrop ____ (g) the setting for a scene or situation

B True or False

(　　) 内の適切な単語を選び英文を完成しなさい。次にその英文が本文の内容に合っていれば T (True)、間違っていれば F (False) を選びなさい。

1. Rooms at many love hotels in Japan are only a little smaller (**as / than**) many apartments in big cities. **[T F]**
2. No-tell motels are similar (**to / with**) love hotels, but not as numerous or luxurious. **[T F]**
3. According to the author, love hotels can be an attractive (**alternately / alternative**) to regular hotels. **[T F]**

2 Conversation

A Listen and Write 69

次の会話を聞いて空所に単語を書きなさい。

W: I can't believe it. Nothing's available!
M: What do you mean?
W: All the hotels are [1](　　　　　) over the long weekend. We have nowhere to stay.
M: Have you [2](　　　　　) looking at a love hotel?
W: What? Aren't they for … you know … secret rendezvous and other [3](　　　　　)?
M: Not at all these days. Some are just like [4](　　　　　) hotels with a little more … character.
W: Ha ha. Well, it does sound interesting, and there is nothing else available.

B Listen and Choose 70

質問を聞いて空所に単語を書き、最も適切な答えを (A) ～ (C) から選びなさい。

1. What is the woman (　　　　　)(　　　　　)?
(A) Accommodations for the long weekend.
(B) A flight home.
(C) Something to do over the long weekend.

2. Why (　　　　　) the man (　　　　　) a love hotel?
(A) Because all the rooms at regular hotels are reserved.
(B) Because he thinks it is no longer available.
(C) Because a love hotel is not too expensive.

3 Text Completion

次の文章を読んで、空所に入れる最も適切な語句や文を (A) ~ (C) から選びなさい。

Throughout history, the idea that love is a complex emotion has been shared by many cultures around the world. _(1)_ Greek literature identifies four broad categories of love. The first is *eros*, or "sexual love." This _(2)_ the feelings of passion and sexual desire. The second is *philia*, or "brotherly love." This is the feeling between friends and comrades, as well as the love one feels for one's family and community. Similar to *philia* is *storge*, or "affection." This is the love between parents and their children. _(3)_ This is demonstrated in the altruism of people like Mother Theresa.

1. (A) Classic
   (B) Classical
   (C) Classify
2. (A) embodies
   (B) representatives
   (C) was symbolizing
3. (A) Finally, there is *agape*, or "charity."
   (B) There are also many subcategories of love.
   (C) Next, there is *philautia*, or "love of self."

4 Composition

A 日本文を参考にして (　　) 内の語句を正しく並べ替えなさい。ただし文頭に来る語も小文字にしてある。

1. (big / due / in / shortage / the hotel / to) cities in Japan, love hotels are becoming more popular places for foreign tourists, too.
   (日本では大都市のホテル不足のため、ラブホテルは外国人観光客にも人気の場所になってきています)

   ____

2. Love hotels offer their guests many amenities that (could / dream / hotels in the world / no other / of / offering).
   (ラブホテルは、世界の他のホテルが宿泊客に提供するとは夢にも思わない、多くのアメニティを提供します)

   ____

3. In the U.S., certain motels in urban areas (a Japanese love hotel / the same / as / function / often / serve), and are colloquially known as "no-tell motels."
   (アメリカでは、市街地にあるモーテルは、しばしば日本のラブホテルと同じ機能を持ち、俗に「ノーテルモーテル」として知られています)

   ____

B (　　) 内の語句を使って、質問に対する応答文を考えなさい。

1. When choosing a hotel, what is more important to you, cost or location? Why?
   (a priority / I often consider / close to a station)

   ____

2. Non-traditional families, including single-parent families, mixed families, and couples who choose not to get married, have become more common. Do you think these kinds of families will become more or less common in the future? Why?
   (have changed / it was common ... to / are getting divorced)

   ____

Unit 24 Faces of Japan

外国の人には、日本は不思議な国に見えます。超高層ビルや高速鉄道をイメージしたり、ゲームやマンガをイメージしたり、お城や寺院、匠の技による工芸品をイメージしたりします。過去と現在が共存している不思議さや発見を与えてくれるのが日本文化なのです。

1 Reading 71

For many people in the West, Japan is a country of mystery. Some imagine Japan as a country of towering skyscrapers, robots, and futuristic transportation – a place where people put in long working hours in highly organized companies. Others see Japan as a bright and cheerful country where people parade around in outrageous costumes and spend their days playing video games or reading comics. Yet others hold onto the notion that Japan is a country of castles, temples, and *ninjas* – where *geisha* and *samurai* walk hand in hand past wooden shops and outdoor food stalls. Those who get the opportunity to visit Japan soon realize that Japan is none of these and all of these at the same time.

The Japanese aesthetics is fascinating because it reconciles what in the West might be considered separate things. People in the West generally have a binary view of the world, separating things like politics and religion, craft and art, past and present. In Japan, however, these disparate concepts appear to exist simultaneously. Take, for example, the practice of *ikebana* or *bonsai*, which brings the natural and the man-made into harmony, or daily utensils like chopstick holders, which are both functional and decorative. *Netsuke* and wooden hair clasps showcase not only the craftsmen's technical expertise, but also their appreciation of beauty.

In Japan, you can ride on the *shinkansen* through the glare of metropolitan cities on your way to enjoying the tranquil gardens of a centuries-old temple garden. You can stay in a traditional Japanese inn complete with modern amenities like 4K televisions and washlets while wearing a *yukata*, walking on *tatami*, and sleeping on a *futon*.

This permeability of Japanese aesthetics is what, at least for me, makes Japan so intriguing. Even after having lived here for so many years, I still find Japan to be a constant source of wonder and discovery.

Notes **towering skyscrapers**「高くそびえる超高層ビル」 **put in long working hours**「長時間仕事に取り組む」 **hold onto the notion**「考えを持ち続ける」 **walk hand in hand**「手を取り合って歩く」 **food stall**「屋台」 **disparate concept**「異なる概念」 **the man-made**「人工のもの」 **chopstick holder**「箸置き」 **technical expertise**「技術的な技」 **complete with**「～の備わった」

A Vocabulary

次の単語の意味を (a) ～ (g) から選び、下線上にその記号を書きなさい。

1. futuristic ____ (a) a feeling of being grateful for something
2. outrageous ____ (b) a person who makes beautiful objects by hand
3. functional ____ (c) designed to have a practical use
4. craftsman ____ (d) extremely interesting; fascinating
5. appreciation ____ (e) quiet and peaceful
6. tranquil ____ (f) very modern
7. intriguing ____ (g) very strange or unusual

B True or False

(　　) 内の適切な単語を選び英文を完成しなさい。次にその英文が本文の内容に合っていれば T (True)、間違っていれば F (False) を選びなさい。

1. People in the West have many different ideas of (**that / what**) Japan is like. **[T F]**
2. Japanese aesthetics combines many ideas (**that / whose**) people from Western countries feel are separate. **[T F]**
3. After living in Japan for a long time, the author feels that Japan has become (**bored / boring**). **[T F]**

2 Conversation

A Listen and Write 72

次の会話を聞いて空所に単語を書きなさい。

M: What are you reading?
W: A book about Japanese culture.
M: But you're Japanese. Why would you read a book about your 1(　　　　) culture?
W: Do you remember when I went to America for a 2(　　　　　　) last month?
M: Yeah. You said you had a really 3(　　　　) time.
W: I did, but people 4(　　　　) asking me about Japan and Japanese culture. Sometimes, I couldn't answer their questions, and I realized that there was a lot I didn't know about my own country.

B Listen and Choose 73

質問を聞いて空所に単語を書き、最も適切な答えを (A) ～ (C) から選びなさい。

1. (　　　　)(　　　　)(　　) book is the woman reading?
(A) She is reading a book about America.
(B) She is reading a book about Japan.
(C) She is reading a book about homestays.

2. (　　　)(　　) the woman (　　　　　　) about Japanese culture?
(A) Because her friends asked her to read the book.
(B) Because she wants to write her own book about Japanese culture.
(C) Because she wasn't able to answer some questions about her own culture.

3 Text Completion

次の文章を読んで、空所に入れる最も適切なものを (A) ～ (C) から選びなさい。

The basic definition of "culture" is the characteristics and knowledge of a group of people, including their language, religion, cuisine, social habits, music, and arts. However, culture is more than _(1)_ is produced or created by a group of people. Culture can also be seen as the way people interact with _(2)_. Culture includes how people perceive the world around them and how they learn to socialize. It also includes how a group of people identify themselves and how that identity develops through social interactions. When looked at in this way, _(3)_.

1. (A) that
   (B) which
   (C) what

2. (A) all together
   (B) each other
   (C) one after another

3. (A) cultural differences can cause conflict between groups of people
   (B) culture has a much broader definition
   (C) culture is far less complicated than we think

4 Composition

A 日本文を参考にして(　　)内の語句を正しく並べ替えなさい。ただし文頭に来る語も小文字にしてある。

1. Only by (can / grasping / not only / the Japanese spirit / understand / we) Japan's past and present, but also its future.
   (日本人の心を把握することによってのみ、私たちは日本の過去と現在だけでなく、未来も理解することができます)

   ____

2. (arts and crafts / at / is / Japanese / the aesthetic / the heart of) of *wabi-sabi*, the idea that beauty sits within imperfections.
   (日本の美術工芸の中心には、美は不完全さの中にあるという考えである「わびさび」の美意識があります)

   ____

3. Cherry blossoms, called *sakura*, are a symbol of (are / beautiful / idea / the Japanese / that / things) generally short-lived.
   (「サクラ」と呼ばれる桜の花は、美しいものは概して短命であるという、日本人の考えの象徴です)

   ____

B (　　)内の語句を使って、質問に対する応答文を考えなさい。

1. What Japanese tradition is the most important to you? Why?
   (preserve the tradition of / are pleasantly surprised by)

   ____

2. Many people say that traditional Japanese values are disappearing. Do you agree or disagree? Why?
   (are influenced by / On the other hands, / have become interested in)

   ____

Enjoying Different Cultures [B-917]
グローバル化の中で学ぶ日本文化

1　刷　2021 年 1 月 30 日
3　刷　2024 年 2 月 14 日

著　者　アーノルド・アラオ　Arnold Arao
三原　京　Kei Mihara
巳波　義典　Yoshinori Miwa
木村　博是　Hiroshi Kimura

発行者　南雲一範　Kazunori Nagumo
発行所　株式会社　南雲堂
〒162-0801　東京都新宿区山吹町361
NAN'UN-DO Publishing Co., Ltd.
361 Yamabuki-cho, Shinjuku-ku, Tokyo 162-0801, Japan
振替口座：00160-0-46863
TEL: 03-3268-2311（営業部：学校関係）
03-3268-2384（営業部：書店関係）
03-3268-2387（編集部）
FAX: 03-3269-2486

編集者　加藤　敦
組版・印刷　啓文堂
装　丁　N スタジオ
検　印　省　略
コード　ISBN978-4-523-17917-7　C0082

Printed in Japan
落丁・乱丁，その他不良品がございましたら，お取り替えいたします。

E-mail nanundo@post.email.ne.jp
URL https://www.nanun-do.co.jp/